AUSTRALIAN ARMY

CW00671043

EXPLORING GALLIPOLI

AN AUSTRALIAN ARMY BATTLEFIELD GUIDE

LIEUTENANT COLONEL GLENN WAHLERT

ARMY·HISTORY·UNIT

PROTECTING ARMY HERITAGE
PROMOTING ARMY HISTORY

©Copyright Army History Unit
Campbell Park Offices (CP2-5-166)
Canberra ACT 2600
AUSTRALIA
(02) 6266 4248
(02) 6266 4044 – fax
Copyright 2010 © Commonwealth of Australia

First edition 2008
Second edition 2011

National Library of Australia Cataloguing-in-Publication entry
Author: Wahlert, Glenn.
Title: Exploring Gallipoli/ Glenn Wahlert.
Edition: 2nd ed.
ISBN: 9780980475357 (pbk.)
Series: Australian army campaigns series; 4.
Notes: Includes bibliographical references and index.
Subjects: 1. World War,1914-1918–Battlefields-Turkey-Gallipoli-Guidbooks.
2. World War, 1914-1918–Campaigns-Turkey-Gallipoli. 3. Australia-History-Military. I. Australia. Dept. of Defence. Army History Unit. II. Title. (Series: Australian Army Campaign Series)
Dewey Number: 940.426

Printed in Malaysia

Title page image: Anzac Cove (Painting by Frank Crozier)

CONTENTS

Lone Pine Memorial

SECTION 1: HOW TO USE THIS BOOK

This book aims to provide practical touring information for the independent traveller to Gallipoli, doubling also as a handy guide to the fascinating First World War Anzac battlefields. While there are a number of existing guidebooks on Turkey, none of these provides adequate detail on both the battlefields and the attractions of the surrounding area while simultaneously including an overview of the campaign and detail on the events that marked specific locations. This book aims to both supplement the existing stock of guidebooks and fill the gaps. It is not intended as a comprehensive history of Gallipoli. For those wishing to research the detail of the campaign, specific battles or locations, please refer to the Bibliography provided at the end of this book.

Australians and New Zealanders are justifiably renowned as global wanderers. Among the tourists picking their way through the ancient sites of Rome, sipping a G&T in Raffles, or shopping in Bloomingdales in Manhattan, it is not unusual to detect the distinctive Australian accent piercing the buzz of the crowd. This is particularly the case on the Gallipoli Peninsula where every year literally thousands of Australians and New Zealanders attend the dawn service at the North Beach commemorative site. Throughout the year, Aussies and Kiwis of all ages wander the battlefield or frequent the numerous bars and cafés at either Çanakkale or Eceabat processing through the country in a steady stream. In the week before Anzac Day the stream becomes a torrent and the usual patter of Turkish is drowned in the increasing burble of strine.

There is no doubt that Turkey is increasingly becoming a major drawcard for antipodean tourists. It is financially affordable and, given its location on the crossroads of Europe and Asia, offers the traveller a stunningly diverse range of experiences: beautiful beaches, thousands of years of history (including two of the seven ancient wonders of the world), exotic food and a mild climate (at least for most of the year). Add to this the truism that the Turks are among the friendliest people in the world (with the possible exception of Istanbul's cabbies), and the fact that the Gallipoli Peninsula lies on one of the most popular travel routes through Turkey, and the country quickly earns a position on the average globetrotter's list of great places to visit in a lifetime.

1

Turkish troops observing the Australian front line at Gallipoli. *(AWM A05299)*

For the average Australian tourist, a visit to Turkey remains affordable, although it is not as cheap as it once was. The alert traveller can still find the odd bargain, although haggling is an absolute necessity. The western side of Turkey (where the battlefields are located) is generally regarded as just as safe as most European cities. Despite this, intending visitors are strongly urged to check the Department of Foreign Affairs and Trade's travel advisories prior to departure, paying particular attention to the section on safety and security.

As a final note, while this guide provides sufficient information on

hotels and tourist sites in Istanbul to equip the traveller for a short stay, this book is mainly focused on the Gallipoli area. Visitors planning a longer stay in exotic Istanbul, or a journey to other Turkish cities and towns, should invest in one of the better known guidebooks on Turkey, such as The Lonely Planet's *Turkey* (www.lonelyplanet.com) or Frommer's *Turkey* (www.frommers. com). Those Gallipoli visitors who are keen to spend more time than suggested in this book, or to research the British sites at Helles, Krithia and Suvla in more detail, are advised to consult one of the recommended tour books detailed in the Bibliography.

An Australian sniping team looking for targets. *(AWM A05765)*

SECTION 2: SOME BASIC FACTS

WHY DO I NEED A GUIDEBOOK TO THE BATTLEFIELDS?

The Anzac area at Gallipoli is unique among battlefields. While large areas over which the British and French fought have been returned to farmland or villages, the rugged, steep cliffs that both shocked and challenged the waves of Australians and New Zealanders in 1915 remain largely untouched. One can still walk through Monash Valley and spot the Turkish sniper locations or stand in a trench-line at The Nek or Lone Pine and see just how close 'Johnnie' Turk actually was. And it is still common to trip over a piece of shrapnel, find bullets and cartridge cases sticking out of the dirt and, sadly, even uncover human remains.

A reliable guidebook, or an informed guide, should be able to draw the attention of the visitor to all of this and more. There is so much to see that the unwary traveller is likely to miss half of the key locations (such as the lovely Shrapnel Valley and Shell Green cemeteries and the magnificent views from Plugge's Plateau) and waste time wandering aimlessly. Those eight months of the peninsula campaign were so extraordinarily eventful that a quick drive around the area cannot do the location justice or provide the visitor with a sense of the sacrifice made by so many fellow Australians.

Shell Green Cemetery.

The view north from Plugge's Plateau towards Suvla.

DO I NEED A GUIDE?

Travellers who have only half a day to tour the area should take one of the suggested guided tours (see Section 13, *Guided Tours*) and use this book to supplement the tour. While the guides are generally good, they can sometimes provide a distorted view of the campaign, perpetuate some of the old myths of the battles and, due to time constraints, will not visit all of the key locations. Those who have longer than half a day and ready access to a car are strongly urged to take their own tours using this book to plan the route. Cheap rental cars are available in the area for day hire, or travellers may negotiate a day's hire of a cab (see *Section 13, Travel around Gallipoli*).

HOW MUCH TIME DO I NEED?

Half a day will provide a quick overview of Anzac and enable the traveller to pay a short visit to some of the key sites. However, a full day is required for those who wish to include some of the optional walks and leave the main tourist trails. For those who boast a keen interest in the events of Gallipoli and who are not hamstrung by time constraints, two to three days should be sufficient to allow coverage of most, if not all, of the suggested locations. An additional day is necessary to visit the British sites and memorials at Suvla, Krithia and Cape Helles. Many visitors spend a week in the area. Others complete an organised half-day tour, then

5

return to spend a whole day walking the trails, fossicking in the ravines, spending time at those locations the tour missed or at those spots they want to examine in more detail. Travelling the standard route recommended in this guide will take the average visitor around five to six hours in a car. The optional walks and locations will add an additional half to one full day, depending on which walks are chosen and the pace of walking. A full day is required for those who plan to walk the route and visit only the key sites.

HOW DID THE BATTLEFIELD PLACE-NAMES ORIGINATE?

At the time of the landing, maps were in short supply. Those that did exist had no English names for the topographical features, and few even had Turkish identifiers. This added to the confusion experienced by both the Anzacs and the Turks on that first day. Eventually, however, names were invented to aid navigation around the complex geography of Anzac Cove. Many places were named after individuals who had distinguished themselves there or were otherwise associated with the place. For example, Pope's (Lieutenant Colonel Harold Pope), Courtney's (Lieutenant Colonel Richard Courtney), Steele's (Major Thomas Steele) and Quinn's Posts (Major Hugh Quinn) were all named after

key commanders whose troops occupied these areas. Other locations or features were named after events associated with them, such as Shell Green (due to the frequency with which it was shelled), Sniper's Ridge (frequented by Turkish snipers) or Battleship Hill (where the guns of the Royal Navy's ships destroyed a Turkish attack). While some places were not named until after the campaign, all key locations had local names that quickly became familiar. This assisted in the movement of stores and troops and in avoiding confusion during the planning of an attack. The place-names used in this book are those most commonly referred to in the current maps of the area.

GELIBOLU OR GALLIPOLI?

The Turkish town of Gelibolu is *not* Gallipoli. Despite what the guide in Istanbul might insist, Gelibolu is some 60 kilometres from the battlefield and, while a pretty and charming town, is not recommended as an accommodation base from which to visit the battlefields. Gallipoli is named for the jutting finger peninsula where the fighting took place in 1915 and is known to the Turks as the Gelibolu Peninsula. This area of Turkey, including the narrow section of the Dardanelles directly opposite Çanakkale (the Narrows or Çanakkale Straits), has been a battleground for over 3,000 years.

View across the straits from Çanakkale at sunrise.

TURKEY OR THE OTTOMAN EMPIRE?

The Turkish nation was founded in 1923. During the First World War, the Anzacs actually fought against the Ottoman Empire. This empire emerged in the late thirteenth century and reached its zenith at the end of the sixteenth century. From this time on, the political fortunes of the empire were mixed and, by the outbreak of the First World War, the Ottoman Empire was in serious decline, although it still held territory in Syria, Palestine, Arabia and Mesopotamia. With the Treaty of Versailles in 1919, the Ottoman Empire lost much of its territory, reduced in size to the boundaries of its Turkish homeland. Political change championed by Mustafa Kemal, famous for his command of the Ottomans against the Anzacs at Gallipoli, saw the rise of the modern Republic of Turkey in 1923. For ease of reference, this book uses the words 'Turkey' and 'Turk' in place of 'Ottoman Empire' and 'Ottoman'.

WHO FOUGHT AT GALLIPOLI?

The Australians and New Zealanders who served in the nine-month campaign at Gallipoli were members of the Australian and New Zealand Army

Corps (ANZAC). The Australians formed an all-volunteer force, and joined for a wide variety of reasons. These reasons included employment, travel, excitement and, arguably most importantly, a sense of duty. Today, many Aussies and Kiwis believe that their compatriots were alone in fighting the Turks at Gallipoli. In fact, there was a substantially larger British force and a wider variety of nationalities than those that feature in the popular conception. Apart from the Anzacs, other members of the British Empire whose soldiers fought at Gallipoli included Ceylon, India, Nepal and Newfoundland. In addition, France contributed substantial naval and army support, with regiments from Algeria, Morocco and Senegal. Russian, Syrian and Palestinian Jewish refugees also participated, as the presence of the Zion Mule Corps attests. On the other side, a small but valuable (at least to the Turks) team of German officers, advisers and planners provided crucial support to the Turkish Army.

HOW MANY FOUGHT AND DIED AT GALLIPOLI?

Approximately 480,000 Allied (mainly British, Australian, New Zealand and French) soldiers fought in the short campaign, along with some 500,000 Turks. The Australian contingent numbered around 50,000. British casualties (including Imperial forces) exceeded 140,000, including over 21,850 Australians and 7,553 New Zealanders. The remains of over 14,000 Commonwealth soldiers have never been found. Significantly, French casualties at Gallipoli were greater than those of the combined Anzac force (around 30,000), yet most Australians and New Zealanders know little about the French contribution to the campaign. On the opposing side, no-one, not even the Turks themselves, knows the true casualty figure for the Turkish Army. Estimates place this figure at over 250,000.

WHY WAS GALLIPOLI IMPORTANT?

The Dardanelles (also known as the Hellespont at the time of the First World War) is actually a narrow strait connecting the Mediterranean and Aegean seas to the Mamara and Black Seas. It is narrowest directly opposite the town of Çanakkale (about 1.4 kilometres across) which, consequently, acquired enormous strategic importance in the protection of Turkey's capital, Constantinople (now Istanbul). The ancient city of Troy was located near the entrance to the Dardanelles and gained its wealth by taxing the trading ships entering the strait. In 481 BC the army of King Xerxes the First of Persia crossed the

Dardanelles near Çanakkale, followed 150 years later by Alexander the Great. Throughout the Byzantine period (from the fourth to the fifteenth century) the Dardanelles were heavily used and, consequently, fought over by more armies than history can record, including the crusaders. By the early Ottoman period (fourteenth century), the villages on either side of the Narrows (Çanakkale, Eceabat and Kilitbahir) had been heavily fortified and the passage along the Dardanelles and, consequently, through the entrance to Constantinople, tightly controlled.

Çimenlik Castle, Çanakkale.

HOW LARGE IS THE BATTLEFIELD AREA?

As the crow flies, the Anzac battlefield is about 6.5 kilometres long (from the Gaba Tepe Information Centre in the south to the 7th Field Ambulance cemetery in the north) and around 3.5 kilometres wide (from Ari Burnu in the west to the heights of the New Zealand memorial at Chunuk Bair). With the inclusion of the British, French and Turkish sites, the area is over 35 kilometres long (from Suvla Bay in the north to the Cape Helles memorial) and 10 kilometres wide (from Ari Burnu to Eceabat).

9

GALLIPOLI PENINSULA

1 ■ North Beach
2 ■ Ari Burnu Cemetery
3 ■ Anzac Cove
4 ■ Shrapnel Valley Cemetery
5 ■ Plugge's Plateau Cemetery

6 ■ Shell Green Cemetery
7 ■ Lone Pine Memorial
8 ■ Johnston's Jolly Cemetery
8a ■ 4th Bn Parade Ground Cemetery
8b ■ Courtney's & Steele's Cemetery

9 ■ Quinn's Post Cemetery
10 ■ Turkish Memorial
11 ■ The Nek
12 ■ Walker's Ridge Cemetery
12a ■ Russell's Top

12b ■ Baby 700 Cemetery
13 ■ Chunuk Bair
13a ■ The Farm

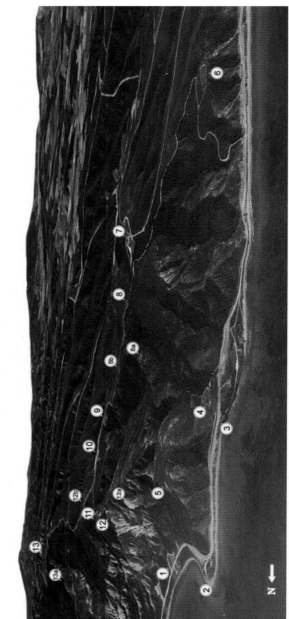

The Anzac battlefield. *(Image by Mark Wahlert)*

WHEN WAS THE FIRST ANZAC DAY COMMEMORATION?

Anzac Day was first commemorated on 25 April 1916, one year after the original landing, when church services were held in Melbourne, Brisbane and London. In 1923, encouraged by the newly formed Returned Servicemen's Association (now the Returned Services League, or RSL), each Australian state gazetted 25 April as a public holiday. Anzac Day veterans' marches first occurred in 1925, with the first official dawn service held at Sydney's Cenotaph in 1927. While an Anzac Day beach service was first held at Gallipoli in 1925, these did not become popular until the 1980s. Today, thousands of Australians and New Zealanders attend the Anzac Day service at the commemorative site at North Beach (Stand 1).

WHO LOOKS AFTER THE ANZAC CEMETERIES?

The Commonwealth War Graves Commission (CWGC) was created in 1917 to establish and maintain permanent cemeteries for all Commonwealth forces. Each member of the Commonwealth contributes to its running costs. The CWGC base near North Beach ensures that the 31 Allied cemeteries at Gallipoli (six at Helles, four at Suvla and 21 at Anzac) are meticulously maintained. The names of those who have no known grave are recorded on one of the 'memorials to the missing'. The Australian memorial to the missing is located at Lone Pine (or at the Helles memorial for those killed in the Second Battle of Krithia). The New Zealand memorials lie at Chunuk Bair, Hill 60, Lone Pine and Twelve Tree Copse.

WHERE ARE THE TURKISH CEMETERIES?

There are no large Turkish military cemeteries on the Peninsula, although there are numerous memorials. The key Turkish memorials are the Çanakkale Martyrs' Memorial at Morto Bay, Cape Helles (near 'S' Beach), the Turkish Soldier's Memorial on Chunuk Bair (Stand 13) and the memorial and open-air mosque for the *57th Regiment* near Quinn's Post (Stand 9). There are also a number of Turkish memorials and small cemeteries on the Asian shore of the Dardanelles, testament to the emphasis Turkish history places on the victory of the Turkish Navy on 18 March as opposed to the subsequent fighting on the Peninsula. A full list of the war cemeteries and memorials on the Gallipoli Peninsula can be found at http://en.wikipedia.org/wiki/List_of_war_cemeteries_and_memorials_on_the_Gallipoli_Peninsula

Turkish *57th Regiment* Memorial.

HOW CAN I LOCATE A PARTICULAR GRAVE?

The CWGC has an excellent website at www.cwgc.org The site will allow a search of the CWGC database of 1.7 million men and women of the Commonwealth forces who died during the two world wars and the 23,000 cemeteries, memorials and other locations worldwide where they are commemorated. Cemetery plans describing the cemeteries at Gallipoli are available online to aid in the location of a specific grave or memorial.

WHY ARE VISITORS STILL FINDING HUMAN REMAINS AT GALLIPOLI?

The vast majority of those killed at Gallipoli received no formal burial. While the Australians and New Zealanders constructed numerous cemeteries during the campaign, for various reasons, including inaccessibility, many men were left unburied by the time of the withdrawal. War Graves staff first came to Gallipoli in 1919 to construct new cemeteries and inter those Allied soldiers left on the battlefield; however, the ravages of time and the course of the original battle, meant that many men remained missing. Among the Australian casualties, for example, 61% have no known grave, while for the New Zealanders this figure is even higher at 78%. Add to this the fact that the Turkish government did not establish formal cemeteries for their fallen following the war, and the argument that the entire battlefield area should be considered one vast burial ground gathers strength.

Skull unearthed by rain at Lone Pine.
Note the distinct puncture mark at the base of the skull, most likely caused by a projectile.

WHAT SHOULD I DO IF I FIND ANY REMAINS?

All visitors to the Gallipoli National Park should note that it is illegal to dig for artifacts or remains in the park. Occasionally, however, a bone fragment may work its way to the surface through the effects of weather and erosion. If remains are sighted, the CWGC's advice is that the fragment should simply be re-buried. Should more substantial remains be located, visitors are asked to mark the spot and immediately report the find to the Commission's office in Çanakkale, telephone number +90 (0)286 217 1010.

Gallipoli is one large cemetery. Outside those buried in the numerous cemeteries and memorials at Anzac, there are literally tens of thousands for whom there is no known grave (including more than 86,000 Turks). This makes the entire battlefield one vast burial ground. For this reason, due respect should be shown while walking this hallowed ground. In 2006, while walking behind Lone Pine, I discovered human remains that had been uncovered by recent rains. I reported the find to the local CWGC staff and the remains were quickly and respectfully buried in a less conspicuous location.

WHO WAS MUSTAFA KEMAL?

Mustafa Kemal, or Kemal Atatürk (meaning Father Turk), is revered throughout modern Turkey as an immortal hero and an extraordinary leader. In all public offices, bus stops, banks and businesses, a picture of Kemal Atatürk is prominently displayed. Sculptures or monuments to him stand in many parks and public areas, and in front of numerous government buildings. Born in present day Greece, Kemal initially pursued a military career with the Turkish Army in Syria. Fascinated by politics, he joined the Young Turk revolutionary movement which, in 1909, deposed the Sultan. In 1915 he was the commander of the 19th Infantry Division at Gallipoli, the main Turkish reserve at the time of the Anzac landing. Using initiative a good grasp of tactics, Kemal stopped the Anzac breakout, contained them within their small beachhead and thwarted several ambition allied plans to capture the heights of the Sari Bair range. Kemal was the driving force behind the creation of the Republic of Turkey in 1923 and became its first President. He implemented sweeping political, economic and cultural changes in Turkey and is credited with creating a modern, democratic and secular state based on Western principles of governance. More than almost anywhere else in Turkey, Kemal's presence is particularly noticeable in Çanakkale (the largest of the towns near the Gallipoli battlefields). It was at Gallipoli that Kemal played a key role in the defeat of the Anzacs while commanding the *Turkish 19th Division*. Visitors strolling around any of the towns on the Peninsula, or even touring the battlefield, are constantly reminded of Kemal Atatürk's role in driving off the invader.

Mustafa Kemal (AWM P04621_002)

SECTION 3:
THE ORIGINS OF THE GALLIPOLI CAMPAIGN

TURKEY'S ENTRY INTO WORLD WAR I

At the time of the outbreak of World War I in August 1914, Europe consisted of two armed camps: the Central Powers of Germany and Austria-Hungary, and the Triple Entente of Britain, France and Russia. Both camps were committed to their partners through a complex web of alliances. In the period prior to the war, Turkey — or the Ottoman Empire as it was then known — appeared uncommitted. Both Britain and Germany courted Ottoman Turkey, hoping to secure its allegiance. However, a combination of ham-fisted diplomacy by Britain, an opportunistic Germany, and the fact that Russia was a traditional enemy of Turkey, brought Turkey closer to the Central Powers. In October 1914, with Germany's blessing, Turkey closed the Dardanelles to the Triple Entente and raided Russia. Russia responded by declaring war on Turkey, and the remaining Entente powers, Britain and France, followed suit a short time later.

WHY ATTACK TURKEY?

The Allied attack on Gallipoli was, in many ways, a direct consequence of the stalemate in France at the end of 1914, combined with a desire to prop up an ailing ally—Russia. While the German advance on Paris had been halted, neither the French nor the British had been able to turn the tide. The combatants dug in and a seemingly interminable stalemate resulted. The Germans had enjoyed some success on their Eastern Front where they had crippled the Russian army. Once Turkey entered the war on Germany's side, Russia was faced with a new threat—a Turkish advance through the Caucasus.

As the deadlock continued on the Western Front, Britain and France looked for a way to outflank Germany. The British First Lord of the Admiralty (and later Britain's Prime Minister in World War II), Winston Churchill, was a strong advocate of a naval attack on Turkey—the 'soft underbelly of Europe'—as a way of opening a back door into Germany. Indeed, while history regards Churchill as the author of the Gallipoli expedition, the Royal Navy had long regarded an attack on

Turkey as a key means of defending British possessions in Egypt and the Suez (although their own staff papers had shown it an almost impossible task). In the end, Churchill was successful in arguing for a purely naval assault to force the Dardanelles and allow the Royal Navy to threaten Constantinople. This action, or so it was believed, would immediately result in Turkey's surrender and the gaining of access to the Black Sea and a secure supply route to Russia.

In February 1915, Lord Kitchener, Britain's Secretary of State for War, issued instructions for the Dardanelles operation and alerted British forces in Egypt, along with the newly arrived Australian and New Zealand troops, for possible employment in support. The British planners firmly believed that the Turks would be easily defeated and that no ground forces would be necessary, except to occupy Turkish coastal forts and Constantinople itself.

Replica of the *Nusrat*. The *Nusrat* was a small Turkish mine-laying vessel that played an important role in the Turkish naval victory over the combined Allied fleet in March 1915.

NAVAL ATTACK

The guns of the Royal Navy and French navy ships first fired on the Turkish forts on 19 February 1915. The initial attack involved about seventy warships, with a quick victory expected. However, a combination of strong Turkish resistance, poor Allied gunnery, and bad weather meant that it was a week before even the outer forts of Seddülbahir and Kumkale could be taken. Worse was to come for the Allies. On 18 March, having failed to silence the Turkish mobile artillery batteries or even the forts further along the straits, the Allied navies opened a major naval assault with sixteen battleships. This was designed to be a knockout punch. Instead, it turned into one of Britain's worst naval disasters. Several ships were hit by Turkish guns and six capital ships struck undetected mines. Admiral

A couple of 'diggers' train in Egypt before the Gallipoli campaign. Note that the nickname 'digger' actually was not attributed to the Australian soldier until they moved to France in 1916. *(Artwork by Jeff Isaacs)*

De Robeck, the Commander of the East Mediterranean Squadron, withdrew his ships and advised London that troops were required to capture the Peninsula and silence the Turkish guns before his ships could make passage through the Dardanelles.

It is difficult to appreciate today how immense a victory this was for the Turks. The combined French and Royal navies represented a formidable force and Turkey was expected to capitulate quickly; the notion of a Turkish victory was simply unthinkable. This victory is still commemorated each March in Çanakkale, and the various small towns and villages in the area. Modern-day tourists are reminded frequently of this victory in displays of Turkish national pride.

A replica of the celebrated Turkish vessel, *Nusrat*, rests in the grounds of the Çanakkale military museum. The *Nusrat* was a small mine-laying warship that played a crucial role in the defeat of the Allied navies in 1915. Visitors taking the ferry across to Çanakkale from Eceabat for the first time should look towards the hills north of the town. There, prominently cut into one of the hills is the simple inscription '18 Mart 1915'. This is the date celebrated by the Turks as marking their victory at Gallipoli: 18 March 1915—a full five weeks before the Anzacs had even landed.

THE ARMY OPTION

Having been warned out for operations by General Haig, the British Army in Egypt had already planned an assault on the Dardanelles within days of the naval defeat. In March 1915, General Sir Ian Hamilton was appointed to command the newly formed Mediterranean Expeditionary Force. This force consisted of around 75,000 troops from Britain, France and the largely untested armies of Australia and New Zealand. There were also around 1,600 horses, donkeys and mules.

The defeat of the Allied navies was regarded as extremely embarrassing by both the British and French commanders. In their haste to capture the Peninsula and allow a face-saving resumption of naval operations, General Hamilton and his staff committed a number of grave errors. There were few maps of the areas to be assaulted and intelligence on the enemy was sparse to non-existent. Because no overall commander had been appointed, cooperation between the Naval Commander, De Robeck, the Force Commander, Hamilton, and the General Officer Commanding Egypt, Sir John Maxwell, was poorly coordinated and the planning marked by confusion, turf protection and indecision. By far the most significant flaw, however, was the contempt in which the Allied planning staff held the Turks. Little effort was made to deceive Turkey on the nature of Allied intentions, effectively robbing the Allies of any vestige of strategic surprise. Security in Egypt was poor and it was obvious to all that a major campaign was about to be launched and that the target was Turkey. Indeed, the *Egyptian Gazette* in Cairo announced the arrival of the various contingents and openly discussed the coming campaign. Mail to some Allied troops was already being addressed to the 'Constantinople Expeditionary Force'. While it was accurately assumed that the Turkish Army was poorly trained, equipped and led, no allowance was made for the fact that Turkey had over a month to prepare for any landing and had acquired an efficient cadre of German officers to help plan her defence.

The Allied plan was simple. It involved a straightforward assault using the British 29th Division to capture the southern tip of the Peninsula around Cape Helles, while the two Anzac divisions (1st Australian Division and the Australian and New Zealand Division) would land further north at Gaba Tepe. The French were to make a diversionary assault at Besika Bay, while the actual landing occurred at Kumkale. The 29th Division was to quickly capture the forts along the southern edge of the Peninsula, while the French would seal the opposite end of the strait. The Anzacs were to protect the British left flank and march inland to cut the Peninsula in two.

THE TURKISH ARMY AT GALLIPOLI

Prior to the disastrous Allied naval attacks in March, any land invasion launched along the Gallipoli Peninsula almost certainly would have been successful. The area was viewed by the Commander of the Turkish *5th Army* as a relatively low priority and was defended by units that were under strength, lacking in almost every type of military equipment, poorly organised for a defensive battle and badly led. Most of the front-line soldiers had only a few rounds of ammunition, were supported by an unreliable supply chain and were forced to wear items of their own civilian clothing to compensate for a shortage of uniforms.

Following the naval attack, however, the Turks appointed German General Liman von Sanders as commander of the defences at Gallipoli in anticipation of the expected land assault. Liman was appalled by the Turks' lack of preparation and the quality of the troops assigned to him. One of his regiments, the *77th*, consisted mainly of Arabs with little or no loyalty to the Ottoman Empire. He had no aircraft to assist with reconnaissance, poor infrastructure, and few transport assets to move, let alone manoeuvre his force, an almost non-existent administrative system to supply it and an ineffective communications network.

Despite the immense obstacles confronting him, he and his staff reorganised the defence of the area, re-equipped and strengthened the *5th Army*, built roads and bridges to move troops and supplies, and devised a strategy to defend the likely landing sites. With such a small force to cover over 150 miles of coastline, Liman could not hope to defend all of the beaches. Consequently, his strategy was to place lookouts above the beaches and hold his main force behind the ridgelines.

'Abdul', how the diggers initially viewed their enemy. *(Artwork by Jeff Isaacs)*

German General Liman von Sanders, Commander-in-Chief of the Turkish Army. *(AWM J00200)*

SECTION 4: THE LANDINGS

THE BRITISH AND FRENCH LANDINGS

The Allied forces were scheduled to land over seven separate beaches. Apart from the planned Anzac landing at 'Z' Beach near Gabe Tepe (a couple of kilometres south of where they actually landed), major landings were also to occur at the tip of the Peninsula at 'V' and 'W' beaches around Cape Helles. These were to be supported by smaller landings at 'X' and 'Y' beaches north-west of Cape Helles, and at 'S' Beach inside the Dardanelles. Additionally, a French force was to effect a diversionary landing on the opposite side of the Dardanelles at Kumkale.

The major British landings around Cape Helles were strongly opposed by infantry and the well-defended fortress at Seddülbahir. As an indication of the ferocity of the fighting, six Victoria Crosses were awarded for bravery at 'V' Beach where three battalions suffered casualties amounting to approximately 70% of their strength. At other locations the landings met little or no opposition. The French 1st Division landing at Kumkale quickly overcame light resistance and, at 'S' Beach, the 2nd South Wales Borderers waded ashore unmolested. Likewise, at 'Y'

View from the beached British transport ship *SS River Clyde*, a few hours after she was beached, showing the ruins of the Seddülbahir Fort. *(AWM A03076)*

Beach, a force of 2,000 men found little opposition and advanced within sight of Krithia village. However, the British commander, General Sir Ian Hamilton, chose to withdraw his troops from the lightly defended beaches and use them to reinforce the mounting disaster at Cape Helles. Within a month, the British regiments around Cape Helles had suffered 20,000 casualties.

LANDING AT ANZAC

The centerpiece, and main focus of the landing, was to be around Cape Helles. The Anzacs were to secure a landing zone further north and, in so doing, force the Turks to commit their sizeable reserves known to be in the area. Should the opportunity arise, they were then to move quickly

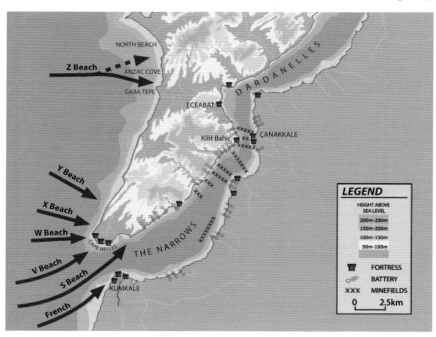

LANDINGS 25 APRIL 1915

■	**Kumkale:**	1st Div (Fr)		**W** ■	**Beach:**	1st Lancashire
S ■	**Beach:**	2nd 5th Wales Borderers		**X** ■	**Beach:**	2nd Royal Fusiliers
V ■	**Beach:**	1st Munsters		**Y** ■	**Beach:**	1st KOSB
		1st Dublin				Plymouth Bn RND
		2nd Hampshires		**Z** ■	**Beach:**	A&NZ Ary Corps

Allied landing beaches at Gallipoli, 25 April 1915. *(Image by Mark Wahlert)*

inland behind the Turkish positions at Cape Helles and cut the Peninsula in two. So as to surprise the Turks, the Anzac landings were not preceded by a preliminary bombardment. However, as dawn broke on 25 April, it was the Australians who were surprised. Instead of the wide beach and open, flat country they had been expecting, they faced steep cliffs, deep gullies and constant sniping from an enemy occupying the high ground.

The first wave of 1,500 Australians from the 3rd Brigade (9th, 10th and 11th Battalions) landed around Ari Burnu (Bee Point), about three kilometres north of their proposed landing point. While it was clear that an error had occurred, it was equally clear what had to be done—the beach had to be secured so that reinforcements and supplies could move in, and the high ground had to be cleared and occupied. Displaying amazing athletic ability, the Australians raced down the valleys and gullies and scaled the heights around their landing areas. Around midday, they were joined by the Kiwis. By then, reinforcements were desperately needed to counter a fierce Turkish counter-attack.

By the end of that first day, the Anzacs had only a tenuous hold on a tiny area of the Peninsula a little over one kilometre wide and two kilometres long. The Turks occupied the second and the third ridges and from these more dominant locations could observe and fire on large areas of the Anzacs' positions. The situation was desperate. A number of the Anzac commanders even considered an immediate withdrawal. They had landed on the wrong beach, had not achieved their objectives and were surrounded by an unexpectedly large and aggressive Turkish force. Already they had suffered about 3,000 casualties with a major attack expected in the morning. However, Sir Ian Hamilton, Commander-in-Chief of the Mediterranean Expeditionary Force, would have none of it and the Anzacs were ordered to dig in and hold.

DID THE AUSTRALIANS LAND AT THE WRONG BEACH?

Controversy has surrounded this question for decades. Many assume that the navy mistakenly landed the first wave of Australians at what became Anzac Cove, nearly three kilometres further north than planned, and that this mistake was caused by currents or a simple error of navigation. However, the Anzac Commander, General Sir William Birdwood, stated in the period following the landings that it had been his intention to land the Australians at Anzac Cove as, while the area was much more rugged than around Brighton Beach, it was less heavily defended. A lie to cover a blunder or a well-concealed plan to deceive the Turks? Certainly there is little evidence to support Birdwood's claim, and much to suggest that it was a simple mistake. None of the senior commanders, for example, appears to have known of any change in landing site. Colonel Sinclair-MacLagan, the commander of the first troops to land (3rd Brigade), was surprised to find that they had landed on the wrong beach. Not even the commander of the 1st Australian Division, General Bridges, appears to have known of the change.

Certainly a landing close to Gaba Tepe was likely to have been well opposed by the Turks as they 'had given a great deal of thought to Gaba Tepe' and had two reserve battalions located nearby. And while some boats were likely to have landed as far north as Anzac Cove, and even North Beach, under the original plan, not all of them were to have beached as far north as they did. To lend some perspective to this landing 'error', almost thirty years later the Americans missed Utah Beach by around 1800 metres during the Normandy landing, and this was after a year of planning.

WHAT WAS THE TURKISH RESPONSE TO THE LANDINGS AT ANZAC?

Facing the Australian landing on 25 April were some 250 men from an infantry company of the *27th Regiment* under the command of Captain Faik. Faik was supported by a company of mountain guns and was responsible for defending the beaches from Gabe Tepe to the north of Ari Burnu. Faik's company headquarters was entrenched at Ari Burnu, with a number of piquets dispersed along the ridges and high ground overlooking likely landing places. The majority of his men were farmers from the Gallipoli Peninsula, Çanakkale or one of a hundred similar villages in the region.

When the first Australians jumped off their boats and waded ashore at around 4.30 a.m. on 25 April, only Faik's infantry was the Turk's first line of defence against the invaders. A runner was dispatched and reinforcements ordered. Ultimately, a combination of the numbers of Australians in the first wave, the fire from the British ships after first light and a shortage of ammunition forced the Turks to withdraw to the next ridgeline.

By mid-morning, the Australians had largely recovered from the initial shock of landing in the wrong place, had killed or chased off most of the enemy on the hills overlooking the beach and, in small, ad hoc groups, were attempting to push on to the third ridge (Gun Ridge). Back at Turkish headquarters confusion and indecision reigned, delaying a coordinated response. In the absence of instructions, the acting commander of the *19th Division*, Lieutenant Colonel Mustafa Kemal, took the initiative and rushed his regiments to reinforce the few Turks left resisting the Australian advance. Arriving late in the morning, Kemal rallied the Turks, stating bluntly, 'I don't order you to attack, I order you to die. In the time it takes us to die, other troops and commanders can come and take our place.' While Kemal rushed to secure the northern heights above the site of the Anzac landings, including Chunuk Bair and Baby 700, Lieutenant Colonel Aker's *27th Regiment* was pushing in from the south. By nightfall Kemal and Aker had stabilised the situation and rebuffed all attempts by the Australians and New Zealanders to push forward.

Turkish soldiers' shelter at Gallipoli. *(AWM A02599)*

END OF DAY 1

By the end of the first day, the Anzacs had achieved few of their objectives. The rough, steep terrain had slowed their progress. Men became lost in the deep, overgrown ravines, and the lack of maps and signalling equipment made it extremely difficult for them to consolidate their positions. Throughout the afternoon Mustafa Kemal, with his knowledge of the terrain and the difficulties the Anzacs would be facing, was able to reinforce his troops and offer strong resistance. By late afternoon he had been joined by the *57th* and *72nd Regiments* and the Turkish counter-attacks had forced the Anzacs off several high points. By nightfall the Anzac position was in jeopardy and a withdrawal was considered. Hamilton, however, refused to countenance a withdrawal and ordered all troops to 'dig, dig, dig!' What the Anzacs and Turks could not have foreseen is that the stalemate that existed from dawn on the second day would remain almost unchanged for the rest of the campaign.

Lieutenant Colonel Kemal observes Australian positions at the end of the first day. *(Artwork by Jeff Isaacs)*

NAVAL SUPPORT

The role of the navy is critical to the success of any amphibious operation. Gallipoli was no exception. The Royal Navy's role was to land and supply the force at Anzac, and provide vital ship-to-shore artillery support. Land-based field artillery was in short supply. Consequently, in the planning for the landings at Gallipoli, the big guns of the Royal Navy were factored in as the force's main source of fire support. While there were a few examples of naval artillery saving the day for the Anzacs, ship-to-shore bombardments proved generally ineffective. The terrain around Anzac suited guns that could fire at a high elevation to hit reverse slope positions, hilltops and deep gullies. The navy's guns, while packing quite a punch, fired on a flat trajectory and could not access many of the Turkish positions, especially after the Turks learned how to position their trench-lines to minimise interference from naval gunfire. Firing off an unstable platform with poor communications to direct the fire, the naval guns could only hit some of the targets they could see from the ship and proved generally inaccurate. This did not bode well for the type of combat that was to feature at Anzac. In numerous places the distance between the two sides was only a few metres. Large high explosive charges which fell indiscriminately around the Anzac positions, and which could not be accurately adjusted, did not bolster the confidence of the hapless Aussies and Kiwis on the ground. Eventually, after three British battleships were torpedoed in May, most of the capital ships were withdrawn to safer waters.

Australian Navy submarine *AE2* at sea. *(AWM H17538)*

SUBMARINE SUCCESS

Within 24 hours of the landing, the Anzacs situation appeared so dire that withdrawal was seriously contemplated. The one piece of good news that passed quickly around the Allied lines via the 'bush telegraph' told of the success of the Australian submarine, *AE2*, commanded by Lieutenant Commander Stoker. The *AE2* had managed to slip past the mines and the submarine nets and gain access to the Dardanelles, the only submarine to have penetrated the Turkish defences at that point. While the *AE2* failed to do any real damage to Turkish shipping and was eventually sunk on 29 April, it gave the Allied armies a much-needed morale boost. Hamilton seized on this news and used it to dismiss any talk of withdrawal.

WHAT WAS THE ATTITUDE OF THE ANZAC SOLDIER TO HIS ENEMY?

Generally, at the time of the commencement of the campaign, the typical Allied soldier thought little of his enemy. It was assumed that the Turkish soldier was a poor fighter and that the Turkish Army would quickly collapse in the face of the superior British and French forces. In the period that followed the landings, however, a level of hatred of the Turk became evident in the writings of the Anzacs. They believed that the Turks had mutilated Allied corpses, mistreated prisoners and used *dum-dum* bullets (an expanding bullet outlawed by the Hague Convention of 1899). However, following the Turkish offensive of 19 May, the Anzac soldiers realised that their early concerns were unfounded and they began to see the Turks as fellow sufferers. Indeed, both the Australians and the New Zealanders began to admire their foe for his courage, devotion to his comrades and proficiency as a soldier. Later in the campaign it was not uncommon for the two sides to exchange gifts and stores by throwing them over to the other's trench.

SECTION 5: AN OVERVIEW OF THE CAMPAIGN

The Anzac campaign at Gallipoli basically unfolded in four phases: the landing and consolidation of positions (April–May); a period of stalemate and trench warfare (June–July); the offensives to break the deadlock (August); and the final resignation and withdrawal (September–December). The next section provides a brief overview of each of these phases. More detail of what actually occurred at specific locations is included in Section 16.

PHASE 1: LANDING AND CONSOLIDATION OF POSITIONS (APRIL– MAY)

While the Anzacs were successful in landing their two divisions, albeit at the wrong location, they were singularly unsuccessful in achieving their initial objectives: occupation of the high ground. At the end of the first day, the Australians and New Zealanders had a very tenuous hold on a tiny slice of land and were surrounded by an aggressive and determined enemy. Despite constant attacks and counter-attacks, neither side made any real progress and the positions they occupied on the morning of 26 April remained largely unchanged. Both sides dug in

and used the time between attacks to fortify their positions. The Anzacs were in a particularly precarious position. By mid-May they had suffered over 6,500 casualties while the Turks had lost 14,000 men.

PHASE 2: STALEMATE (JUNE–JULY)

The failure to gain any real ground or advantage in the numerous attacks and counter-attacks at Anzac, and the similar failures of the British attacks at Cape Helles, meant that little more could be achieved without substantial reinforcement or a fundamental change in strategy. While the generals asked London for more men and equipment, the Anzacs kept digging, reinforcing their positions and communications trenches and basically organising themselves for a long campaign. The summer heat brought a new enemy to both sides—disease. The ubiquitous flies that had been gorging themselves on the rotting corpses and open latrines spread numerous diseases among the troops. Medical facilities could not cope, highlighting yet another deficiency in planning. The Anzacs achieved little during this period. They were holding on by the narrowest of threads and only just keeping the Turks at bay.

The Anzacs dig in. *(Artwork by Jeff Isaacs)*

PHASE 3: AUGUST OFFENSIVES

In August, the landing of two fresh British divisions at Suvla Bay, about eight kilometres north of the Anzac positions, heralded an attempt to break the deadlock at Gallipoli. Following a successful landing, these divisions were quickly reinforced while the Australians and New Zealanders made diversionary attacks at Lone Pine, The Nek and at Chunuk Bair. However, through a combination of poor leadership and inexperience, the landing troops dithered on the beaches and failed to take the initiative and occupy the high ground. By nightfall the Turks had reinforced the area and an attack led by Mustafa Kemal saw the British fall back in disarray. By 10 August, Kemal's troops dominated the Suvla area and any hope of a British success at Gallipoli evaporated.

PHASE 4: RESIGNATION AND WITHDRAWAL (SEPTEMBER–DECEMBER)

The failure of the August offensives to substantially alter the fortunes of the occupying Allied force, and the consequential reluctance of London to send more troops, brought renewed consideration of the prospect of evacuation. Britain was now fighting a war on four fronts: France, Africa, Mesopotamia and Gallipoli. In October, after Australian journalist and future newspaper tycoon Keith Murdoch managed to smuggle out reports of the terrible conditions on Gallipoli which criticised Hamilton in particular, London replaced Hamilton with Lieutenant General Charles Monro. Monro quickly assessed the situation at Gallipoli and concluded that evacuation was the only option. Lord Kitchener, the British Secretary of State for War, visited the front in November and agreed with Monro. As if confirming his assessment, casualties caused by conditions at the front peaked sharply, with 16,000 Allied troops treated for frostbite in that month alone.

Between the 10th and 20th of December, over 80,000 troops and 200 guns were evacuated from Suvla and the Anzac positions. This was achieved without a single casualty and without alerting the Turks—a remarkable feat that owed much to Anzac's Chief of Staff, Australian Brigadier Brudenell White. The remaining British positions around Cape Helles were evacuated in late December and early January 1916.

Anzac Cove after evacuation *(AWM G01784)*

WHAT WAS LIFE LIKE AT ANZAC?

While life at Anzac soon became routine, it was always far from easy. Work details to carry water and supplies, the digging of saps (protective trenches), the improvement of fortifications and even bomb-making were a constant drudgery. These work details were subject to relentless enemy shelling and sniping. It was no easier for those manning the forward trenches. While there were lengthy periods of inactivity, these were interspersed with intense combat, sniping, bombing and shelling. In summer the heat was oppressive, and there was little escape from the mud, rain and cold as the season turned. The food was monotonous. Bully beef and hard biscuits formed the basis of the Anzacs' diet. They had to become used to living with open toilets, rotting corpses, dysentery, lice, flies, stress, strain, monotony and danger.

Life in the Anzac trenches. *(Artwork by Jeff Isaacs)*

SECTION 6: OUTCOMES AND CONSEQUENCES

OUTCOMES OF THE CAMPAIGN

The withdrawal from Gallipoli incited major public debates in the UK, Australia and New Zealand. Winston Churchill, whose name is often linked with Gallipoli, defended the campaign and criticised Monro's decision to withdraw, parodying Julius Caesar when he wrote 'He came, he saw, he capitulated.' Churchill soon became a political casualty of the campaign, however, as he was forced to resign along with his First Sea Lord, John Fisher. Other casualties included Generals Hamilton and Stopford (who led the disastrous Suvla Bay landings), whose careers were effectively over. In contrast, Gallipoli 'created' the future leadership of the Australian Army, with officers such as John Monash and Harry Chauvel soon commanding divisions and, later, army corps.

Perhaps the most immediate impact of the Gallipoli campaign was felt by the victor—Turkey. Turkey suffered around 250,000 casualties and, as T.E. Lawrence (renowned as 'Lawrence of Arabia') argued, the 'first line Ottoman Army' was effectively destroyed, assisting both the Arab revolt and Allenby's campaign in Palestine.

However, the Gallipoli campaign also engineered the rise of Mustafa Kemal who later, as Mustafa Atatürk, became the founding father of modern Turkey and remains revered throughout Turkey today.

For Australia and New Zealand, Gallipoli was central to the forging of the Anzac legend and the development of a strong sense of national identity. But the campaign also provided both nations with a palpable sense of the horrific cost of war. Over 30,000 Australians and New Zealanders were direct casualties of the fighting, with most Australian towns losing sons to Gallipoli. The ubiquitous war memorials and rolls of honour in country towns across Australia and New Zealand stand silent testament to this fact. In 1934, the President of Turkey, Mustafa Atatürk, who had commanded a Turkish division opposing the Anzacs at Gallipoli, wrote:

Those heroes who shed their blood and lost their lives . . . You are now lying in the soil of a friendly country. Therefore rest in peace. There is no difference between the Johnnies and the Mehmets to us where they lie side by side here in this country of ours... You the mothers, who sent their sons from far away countries, wipe your tears; Your sons are now lying in our bosom and are in peace. After having lost their lives on this land they have become our sons as well.

Ataturk, 1934

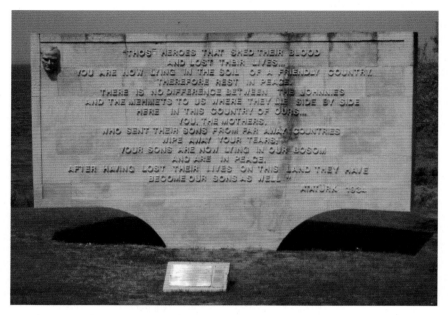

Atatürk's message of reconciliation.

In strategic terms, the Gallipoli campaign also significantly influenced the evolution of amphibious operational thinking among Western armed forces. It provided examples of all four types of amphibious operations: the raid, demonstration, assault and withdrawal. The lessons from Gallipoli were used in the planning for Normandy and the US Marine Corps operations in the South-West Pacific in World War II.

REASONS FOR FAILURE

Debate continues today on the causes of the Allied failure at Gallipoli. The reasons for this failure are undeniably numerous and complex. However, put simply, they can best be summarised as:

Arrogance. The senior Allied planners had dismissed the Turkish Army's ability to resist the might of a combined Allied force. The failure of the naval attack of 18 March should have given them good reason to pause and reflect on the Turk's resilience, adaptability and willingness to fight.

Inadequate preparation. Partly as a consequence of their miscalculation concerning the Turkish Army, the logistics plans (supply, medical, transportation, water sourcing, etc.) for the campaign were grossly inadequate. Indeed, administrative staff were regarded as a 'tedious encumbrance'. Few maps were available below battalion level, and many of those that were issued dated from around 1840. Artillery bombardments often had to be rationed due to shortages of ammunition, and the medical facilities were overwhelmed from the first day. The entire operation was hastily planned and poorly coordinated.

Inexperience. Most senior Allied commanders failed to acknowledge that a revolution in military affairs had occurred in the preceding decade and, consequently, were unable to adapt quickly to modern industrial warfare. Some of the generals made 'suggestions' rather than gave commands to their subordinates (such as Hamilton, the Commander-In-Chief), others tried to ignore even the suggestions (as did Major-General Hunter-Weston, Commander of the British 29th Division) while there were also a few that were simply too old and inexperienced for the tasks assigned (as was 61-year old Lieutenant-General Stopford). Additionally, for the Gallipoli campaign to have even the barest chance of success under the circumstances that unfolded, Hamilton and his staff would have required a level of command and control in joint operations unheard of at that time. Indeed, these techniques took decades longer to develop.

COULD THE GALLIPOLI CAMPAIGN HAVE SUCCEEDED?

Had the Allied navies pressed their attack in March and forced the Straits, or had their land campaign succeeded in at least achieving *some* of their key objectives, Turkey could have been forced out of the war. However a great deal rested on the conduct and success of these elements of the campaign. It was much more likely that Churchill's plan would fail, given the odds arraigned against it from the outset. An absence of intelligence, inadequate and inaccurate maps, poor artillery support, terrible logistics and medical planning, inexperienced and incompetent commanders, untrained troops and unrealistic objectives were but a few of the reasons Gallipoli was doomed to failure.

SECTION 7: PLANNING THE TRIP

PASSPORT AND VISA REQUIREMENTS

Visitors to Turkey should hold a passport that is valid for at least six months. Australian passport holders traveling on a standard tourist (blue) passport may obtain a Turkish entry visa at the airport on arrival. At Istanbul's Atatürk airport, a 'Visitor's Visa' sign is prominently displayed along the concourse from the arrival gateway to the customs line. Similar signs are also displayed in other Turkish airports. A visa costs around €15. Those travelling on an official passport or the passport of another nation are likely to require a visa prior to departure from Australia. Information on visa requirements, application forms and a plethora of other useful information are available at the Turkish Embassy's website www.turkishembassy. org.au Visitors should note that those overstaying their visa period will incur a substantial fine upon departure.

Travel Tip: It is useful to have either € or US$ (not Turkish) currency available to pay for the entry visa at the airport. Prices may vary from time to time, so it is important to check with the Turkish Embassy, Consulate or a travel agent prior to departure.

BEST TIME TO GO

The best time to visit the Gallipoli Peninsula is spring (either April or May) or autumn (particularly September or October), as these periods offer the most comfortable climate. The Turkish high season runs from July to mid-September. This is also the holiday period for the local Turks and so is the peak period for the pleasant seaside villages near Gallipoli, especially Çanakkale. This is the time when accommodation costs are at a premium. European holidays will ensure that Istanbul is also busy, so visitors should plan ahead for any travel during this period.

The Turks regard Anzac Day (25 April) as marking the commencement of their 'backpacker season'. At this time, accommodation and transport can be particularly difficult to find in and around the Gallipoli Peninsula for those visitors not travelling with a tour group or who have not booked well in advance. Even those who have had the foresight to book in advance may find that they have been 'gazumped' and will need to pay an additional 'service charge' to secure their room. In some cases, accommodation may simply have been on-sold to other visitors willing to pay a higher price. The Anzac week is generally packed solid with thousands of visiting Australian and New Zealand tourists of all ages. While prices are higher than at any other time of year, and long queues are in evidence for every single requirement (I mean for absolutely *every*thing), the atmosphere of a joint Australian, New Zealand and Turkish dawn service at the Anzac Commemorative Site at North Beach, and the Australian service at Lone Pine, is emotional and uplifting and one that all Australians should experience at least once in their lifetime.

Travel Tip: Visitors should not simply turn up on the Peninsula for Anzac Day celebrations without first making some arrangements, especially for accommodation. Accommodation, and even ground transport, in the entire region is at a premium at this time. A package deal with a travel company may be the best bet.

Çanakkale Harbour at night.

TRAVEL PERIODS REQUIRING SPECIAL ATTENTION

Anzac Day. Over the Anzac Day period, most of the small towns and villages along the Gallipoli Peninsula burst at the seams with the influx of thousands of Australians and New Zealanders. Prices are high and queues are long. Many regard this as a bad time to visit Gallipoli. Ultimately, a decision to travel at this time will depend on the reason for the visit. Travelling to Turkey around Anzac Day means being prepared to share the Gallipoli experience with thousands of fellow countrymen and women. For those who seek quiet reflection, Anzac Day is not an ideal time to travel.

> **Travel Tip:** For those planning to attend the dawn service at Gallipoli on Anzac Day, be aware that you will probably have to spend the previous night, the 24th, at North Beach as the local police close the park after about 7pm. It is, therefore, advisable to take some warm clothing, a raincoat and a blanket. Hot food and drinks are sold on site.

Ramazan. The holy month of *Ramazan* (known as Ramadan in other Muslim countries) consists of thirty days of fasting, celebration and prayer. As the starting date of *Ramazan* is eleven days earlier than that of the previous year, it is wise to check websites such as www.turkeytravelplanner.com/Religion/ ramazan.html for an accurate date. The devout do not allow anything to pass their lips from sunup to sundown during *Ramazan*—no food, drink or even cigarettes. Non-Muslims are permitted to eat and drink and, in most parts of Western Turkey (such as Istanbul and Çanakkale), visitors will have no difficulty finding a restaurant or café open, although these places are not permitted to serve alcohol. However, in some of the smaller towns on the Peninsula, fewer places will be open during daylight hours. It is also polite to be discrete when eating, drinking or smoking in public during the day. Visitors to Turkey at this time will find the celebrations at night that mark the breaking of the daily fast to be well worth the hunger of the wait.

> **Travel Tip:** It is polite to be discrete when eating, drinking or smoking in public during daylight hours during *Ramazan*. Visitors should take their lead from the local people.

Kurban Bayrami. The most important religious and secular holiday in the Turkish calendar is *Kurban Bayrami*. Celebrations for this feast last around a week and can be quite disruptive to the needs of the unwary tourist. Many services such as banks and post offices will be closed for at least part of this period, and travel and hotel reservations are essential. Travellers should check websites such as www.turkeytravelplanner.com/Religion/ramazan.html, for the dates of this feast as it usually follows *Ramazan*.

Winter. Travelling around Turkey in winter is not impossible for those who are well-prepared. However, it can become very uncomfortable, especially over the period November through to March. Around the Gallipoli Peninsula the temperature can fall as low as ⁻16°C with snow and strong, icy winds not uncommon. The advantage of travelling in winter is the conspicuous absence of other tourists.

Travel Tip: Some hotels and guesthouses close for the winter in Turkey. Those keen to travel at this time of year should book ahead.

CLIMATE

The climate on the Gallipoli Peninsula varies from hot and dry in summer to cold, windy and wet in winter. The average daily temperature in summer is around 23°C while, in winter, it hovers around 4°C. The area is generally quite humid with an average relative humidity of 72%. The highest average rainfall months are December and January (with falls often around 100 mm), while July and August are the driest (generally under 20 mm). Snow regularly falls in January, February and March. This snow will remain on the ground for five to six days on average.

Weather table. *(Image by Mark Wahlert)*

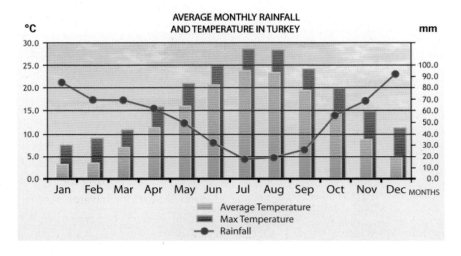

NATIONAL HOLIDAYS

1 January	New Year
23 April	Sovereignty Day and Children's Day
19 May	Youth Day (Atatürk Day)
30 August	Victory Day
29 October	Republic Day

Religious festivals are celebrated according to the Muslim lunar calendar and therefore fall on different dates each year.

MONEY

The Turkish unit of currency is the New Turkish Lira (YTL). The exchange rate fluctuates, but generally sits just under the Australian dollar. Automatic teller machines (ATMs) are plentiful in major cities and tourist areas and credit cards are generally accepted in the larger cities and bigger stores. Small towns are a different matter; many lack the facility to accept either. Local currency can be obtained from banks and exchange bureaux known as *DOVIZ* in Turkish. Banking hours range from Monday to Friday from 8.30 a.m. 12.00 noon, and 1.30 p.m. to 5.00 p.m.

Travel Tip: For convenience, it is advisable to take some Euros (the € is now the most widely accepted foreign currency in Turkey) as, due to past experiences with galloping inflation, prices are often listed in € or US$.

ELECTRICAL APPLIANCES

Turkish electrical appliances use 220 volts/50 cycles and the sockets fit standard European round-pronged plugs.

SAFETY AND SECURITY

The Australian Department of Foreign Affairs and Trade (DFAT) issues a regular travel advisory for Turkey providing detailed information for Australians on safety and security issues as well as other helpful tips. This advice can be found on www.smartraveller.gov.au

Travel Tip: DFAT advises all Australians travelling overseas to register their travel details on the DFAT website at www.orao. dfat.gov.au This information will help authorities locate Australians quickly in an emergency, be it a natural disaster, civil disturbance or a family emergency.

HEALTH

Visitors are strongly advised not to travel without comprehensive medical insurance (including cover for medical repatriation), as private medical treatment in Turkey is very expensive for foreigners.

> **Travel Tip:** Some policies will not cover specified activities such as white water rafting, hang gliding or bungee jumping. Travellers should check any exclusion clauses on their policy documents.

ADDITIONAL TRAVEL TIPS TO ASSIST PLANNING

- Take an electrical adaptor (Turkey uses the standard European round/ 2-prong plug).

- Female visitors should note that tampons (*pak tampon*) can be difficult to purchase outside the larger towns.

- Pack a basic first aid kit including anti-diarrhoea medicine and headache tablets.

- Suntan lotion is essential for those travelling in summer and can be quite expensive to buy in Turkey.

- Remember to take English reading material, unless you are keen to study Turkish.

- All visitors should make copies of passports, insurance policy statements, credit cards, and the particulars of other important documents. One copy of these documents should be carried separately to the originals while a second copy should be left with a relative or friend at home.

- Leave a copy of your travel itinerary with a friend or relative at home and maintain regular contact while overseas.

- Visitors are encouraged to learn a few words of the Turkish language, such as 'hello', 'thank you', and other basic greetings (See www.turkeytravelplanner. com). Those who are serious about learning some Turkish should try the online language classes at http://cali.arizona.edu/maxnet/ tur/ Turkish people genuinely appreciate the efforts of foreigners to communicate with them in their own language.

- Not all toilets have toilet paper. It is advisable to carry a small pack of tissues with you.

SECTION 8: HOW TO GET THERE

Australian recruiting poster, 1915.
(AWM ARTV05167)

TRAVEL TO TURKEY

Travel agents are a good source of advice on the best options for travelling to Turkey. Qantas flies from Australia to the various South-East Asian airline hubs (such as Singapore, Hong Kong and Bangkok) where passengers can change to a Turkish Airlines flight to Istanbul. Emirates and Singapore Airlines also fly to Istanbul from Sydney. Turkish Airlines has a remarkably new fleet of aircraft and provides excellent service.

Visitors travelling from London or elsewhere in Europe obviously enjoy a greater variety of options. Both British Airways and Turkish Airlines fly to Istanbul from London. Cheaper alternatives are available from the continent, including travelling to the Greek Islands and catching a ferry. While Europe-based visitors can also travel overland to Turkey, they are advised to check the Department of Foreign Affairs and Trade website (www.smartraveller.gov.au) for current travel advisories prior to booking, as Turkey has some volatile neighbours.

The relatively new Atatürk International Airport is the recommended entry point into Turkey for those intending to tour the Gallipoli battlefields. This airport is about 25 kilometres from Istanbul's city centre where visitors can spend a few nights sightseeing and resting before travelling on to Gallipoli.

TRAVELLING INTO ISTANBUL FROM THE AIRPORT

Hotel transfers. The most convenient way to travel from the airport to a hotel in Istanbul is via an airport transfer pre-arranged through a travel agent or hotel. While this is more expensive than taking a bus or taxi, most travellers will find that, after a long flight and the confusion of Atatürk International Airport, a fuss-free transfer represents money well spent. Costs for these transfers vary depending on the type of hotel (luxury or budget) and the hotel's location.

Bus. An airport bus service operates from 6.00 a.m. until 11.00 p.m. and costs around AUD$10. The bus stops at the Aksarv terminal and passengers then take either a tram or taxi to the main tourist districts of Sultanahmet or Taksim. There is also an airport bus service that will collect passengers from their city hotel and take them (and their luggage) to the airport. This service costs around AS$9 and details are available from hotel staff.

Train. The Light Rail Transit (LRT) is an efficient and relatively cheap way of getting into Istanbul, and is most convenient for those staying in the Sultanahmet district as the LRT stops close by. Visitors accommodated at Taksim or other districts can take the rail to its final destination at Aksaray and then take a cab to their respective hotels. Trains depart the airport station approximately every ten to fifteen minutes.

Taxi. Taxis are generally plentiful and easy to find at the airport. Travellers should ensure, however, that the cab has a meter and that it is turned on. The fare will depend on the time of hiring (night-time will be cheaper as there is less traffic) and the location of the hotel. As a guide, a taxi should cost around AUD$30 to $40 to drive from the airport to Sultanahmet, and about $10 more to travel to Taksim. Further advice on using taxis in Turkey is provided in Section 9.

Travel Tip: As soon as you exit the Customs arrival hall at Istanbul's airport, you are likely to be set upon by 'gentlemen' in suits offering to arrange transport for you to your hotel, or to even arrange your accommodation. Politely refuse and either hail a taxi at the rank or make your way to the Tourist Information Office.

Self-drive car. Hiring a car at the airport to drive down to Gallipoli is a good idea. Taking it into Istanbul first, is definitely not! Australia has no equivalent to Istanbul's traffic (with the possible exception of New Year's Eve around Sydney Harbour). Attempting to negotiate Istanbul's traffic while trying to find a hotel will most likely waste half a day and raise the visitor's stress levels to boiling point. Travellers who are staying in Istanbul and who intend to eventually drive down to Gallipoli should take a bus or taxi from the airport to their Istanbul hotel. Once they are ready to proceed to Gallipoli, they should return to the airport to collect their hire car before commencing their journey. Further advice on self-drive cars is provided in Section 15.

AIRPORT INFORMATION

Travellers who are unsure of the way to their hotel should check with the Tourist Information Office in the International Terminal (just outside the doors past the baggage claim area). This office can provide up-to-date information on options and costs, and arrange hotel transfers.

Travel Tip: The airport-hotel-airport bus service is cheap and efficient. The main Tourist Information Office will provide details of the service and costs. Travellers are advised to carry the name and address of their hotel in written form to show the driver.

TRAVEL FROM ISTANBUL TO GALLIPOLI

The main regional town of Çanakkale is 325 kilometres south-west of Istanbul. There are three main methods of travel from Istanbul to Gallipoli: air, bus and self-drive car. Each has its advantages and disadvantages and travellers should determine which method best suits their needs.

Air. A regular regional air service operates from Istanbul to Çanakkale. However, it does not always run in winter. If time is at a premium, and cost is not an issue, visitors who wish to fly to Çanakkale can ask their travel agent to confirm that the air service is operating over the period of their visit.

Bus. Bus travel in Turkey is generally simple, cheap, convenient and of a high standard. There are a number of bus companies that make regular runs from Istanbul to Çanakkale, and other towns *en route*. One company worth considering is the *Truva Bus Line* as its buses are modern, clean, air-conditioned, have on-board steward service and run frequently (almost hourly) between Istanbul and Çanakkale, and back. The service costs around AS$30 one way and departs from the main bus terminal of Otogar, which is on the outskirts of Istanbul. Visitors should check timetables, bus companies and fares with their travel agent prior to departing Australia, or consult the Tourist Information Office in the International Terminal. Smoking and the use of mobile phones are generally not permitted on these coaches.

Ferry. A high-speed ferry operates from Istanbul (the Yenikapi fast ferry terminal, a short distance from Sultanahmet) to Bandirma. The journey is a very pleasant two hours across the Sea of Marmara on a modern, fast car ferry. From Bandirma it is a further two and half hour bus trip to Çanakkale. The buses are clean, modern and efficient. From the Bandirma ferry terminal take a taxi or minibus to the main bus terminal (about 3km). The main bus depot in Çanakkale is also about 3km from town. At the time of writing the fares were being reviewed. Check www.ido.com.tr for current fares and timetable.

Car. A self-drive car represents an excellent option for those who are adventurous, courageous in traffic, and able to navigate on the fly. Those travellers who choose to drive are advised to collect their cars at the airport rather than from their Istanbul hotel. From the airport, the drive to Eceabat is around 350 kilometres or four to five hours, depending on the frequency of stops and the state of the traffic.

Travel Tip: Those choosing to hire a car at Istanbul airport and drive to Gallipoli should refer to the advice provided in Section 15 on taking a car. GPS coverage is now available for the Gallipoli area, but not all car hire outlets rent them.

Harem at Topkapi Palace. Istanbul has some fabulous tourist sights and shopping. Visitors should be prepared to do some walking and bargain over prices (see Section 12 for bargaining tips).

SECTION 9: THINGS TO WATCH OUT FOR

Entrance to the Grand Bazaar.

SHOPPING

Turkey offers a wide variety of shopping which will suit most tastes. Reasonable prices can be negotiated for carpets, jewellery, leather goods, clothing, shoes and alabaster. For an unforgettable shopping experience, or simply an exciting visit, try the Grand Bazaar in Istanbul (see Section 11). Note that most shops, including the Grand Bazaar, are closed on Sundays and that the bazaars specialise in 'knock offs' (copies of well-known labels). This means that those *Diesel* jeans, *Lacoste* top and *Armani* T-shirt are not the genuine product, so travellers should not be duped into paying top price. Shoppers should expect to bargain hard—this is a local custom and you should not feel embarrassed or intimidated is doing so. Turkish stallholders expect their customers to bargain. For those keen to try, the simple steps to effective haggling are outlined in Section 12: *Bargaining*. Shoppers should be aware, however, that while bargaining is the norm in the bazaars or when dealing with kerbside vendors, some of the more exclusive shops are fixed-price and staff will not bargain—but these are the exception.

A second word of caution for the novice shopper: visitors should not attend the Grand Bazaar or Spice (Egyptian) Market unless they are ready to be besieged and hassled by literally hundreds of merchants. The best approach is simply to smile, say 'No, thank you', and continue walking. It is not unusual to see tourists in the bazaar being tailed by merchants continuing to try to negotiate a sale.

Travel Tip: It is customary for a stallholder to offer tea to a customer while they discuss a possible sale. However, some may also try to offer *raki*, a strong local spirit. This should be politely declined. Stallholders who offer *raki* may wait for the alcohol to take effect before trying to pressure-sell the customer an expensive item.

Travel Tip: Visitors are advised to check the price of a meal BEFORE they order, particularly if the eating establishment does not appear to have well-marked prices or the prices are unclear. Restaurants and cafés that either have menus in English or pictures of the meal are recommended.

FOOD AND DRINK

Breakfast (kahvalti). Most hotels provide a buffet breakfast included in the room tariff. The usual fare will consist of a combination of cold meats, feta cheese, yoghurt, fruit, boiled eggs, sliced tomato, olives and bread. Hotels do not appreciate guests taking food away to eat later (with the exception of a piece of fruit). While visitors are often initially impressed at the volume of food available at breakfast, after a few days many find themselves craving a simple bowl of *Weet-Bix* or a bacon and egg roll. The Turkish equivalent of such delicacies can be found at the local bakery or pastry shop. These have a wondrous assortment of cheap eats and, although bacon rolls are unlikely to appear on the menu, delicious local pastries such as the *su böreği* (often sold by sidewalk stallholders) are worth trying.

Non-alcoholic drinks. While most visitors have probably heard of Turkish coffee (*Türk kahvesi*), tea (*çay*) is, in fact, the most popular non-alcoholic drink in Turkey. Usually drunk in small, handleless cups, the Turks never mix it with milk but will certainly load it with sugar. Turkish tea is bitter—far more so than its Australian equivalent—but still very refreshing. Coffee comes as either Turkish—black and strong—or as *Nescafe*, coffee with milk. Forget about *cappuccinos* and *lattes*. Tap water can be unsafe to drink and bottled water should be used for both drinking and for cleaning teeth.

Travel Tip: When water is ordered in a restaurant, visitors should ensure that the water brought to them is bottled water and that the bottle is unopened when it is brought to the table.

Turkey's beer and food are excellent but watch out for the *raki*.

towns around the Gallipoli Peninsula, bars and other establishments selling alcohol are plentiful. The most popular Turkish spirit is *raki*, which is similar to Greek *ouzo*. This is a very potent beverage and should be consumed with caution. The local beer, *Efes Pilsen*, is relatively cheap, quite palatable, and should appeal to most Australian beer drinkers.

> ***Travel Tip:*** Visitors who wish to try *raki* should dilute it by about half with water—a practice followed by many of the locals.

Alcoholic beverages. While Turkey is officially a secular state, most Turks are Muslim. Many visitors find that the further east they travel, or the further they are from a major town, the more evident Islam becomes. Certainly in Istanbul and other major towns, including the larger

Water. While most town water is safe, it is best to be cautious, and visitors are strongly urged to drink bottled water and wash all fruit before eating, again using bottled water.

TIPPING

Hotel porter. It is normal practice to tip a hotel porter about one YTL per bag carried.

Restaurants. Tipping in restaurants is more a personal issue; less formal wherever the locals eat, but expected in the more expensive establishments. As always, it is dependent upon the level of service you receive. However, before considering a tip, check what additional charges have been added to your bill. Most will add taxes, but will not usually include the service

charge. In more formal restaurants, visitors should check whether the service charge (*servis ücreti*) has been included. If not, diners may wish to leave about 10%—more or less depending on the standard of service—for the waiter. Adding the 10% to a credit card payment will simply deliver the tip to the proprietor, rather than the staff. Also check whether both a cover charge (*kuver*) and service charge have been added. The charge should be one or the other, but *not both*.

Travel Tip: Some restaurants prey on foreign travellers and will exploit your lack of Turkish language to embellish the bill. Always check your bill—the locals certainly do—and do not be embarrassed to query amounts and items. One useful tip is to keep track of both what is ordered and the price on a piece of paper at the table and check it against the bill. Diners should ensure that the waiter sees them checking as this will assist in avoiding any 'discrepancies' in the final bill.

Taxis. Tipping taxi drivers on short trips usually takes the form of simply rounding up the fare on the meter. For longer journeys, visitors should add one or two YTL. However, if the driver has been particularly helpful and friendly then a larger tip would be appropriate. Passengers who have pre-negotiated a price will not need to tip unless they believe the taxi driver's service to have been exceptional.

Guides. Guides who conduct a half-day to a day's guided tour should receive about 10 YTL if the tour has been well conducted. Guides who provide an excellent service should receive more. For a full-day tour, you may tip as high as 20 or even 30 YTL depending again on the level of service.

Other. Turkish bath masseurs/ masseuses should receive a tip of around four to five YTL prior to the service. Barbers should receive two YTL and hotel room cleaners one YTL per day of stay.

TAXIS

A word of warning! While cabs are plentiful and may often be the best way to get around Istanbul, travellers should be very wary of the tricks Istanbul cab drivers may try. These simple guidelines will help visitors protect themselves from being exploited:

- Ask your hotel staff for advice on what a particular cab fare should be (e.g. from the hotel to the Blue Mosque).

- Upon entering a cab immediately ensure that the driver puts his meter on. If he refuses, or complains that the meter is broken, either leave the cab or negotiate a fare BEFORE departure. Under no circumstances allow the cab to drive off without first having negotiated a fare or ensuring the meter is on. If all else fails, demand that the driver pull over and leave his cab. You may find that his 'broken' meter miraculously repairs itself.

- Check the meter displays the correct tariff - *Gündüz* during the day, and *Gece* at night.

- Be very clear on what notes and amount you give the driver. Some cabbies like to prove that the hand is quicker than the eye and will vow that they were given a five YTL note rather than a fifty YTL (known as a 'bait and switch' routine). Passengers travelling in pairs should have a friend watch the payment process (taking careful note of the actions of the driver).

- Do not accept help from a porter to either carry bags or hail a cab at airports or bus depots unless the amount he intends to charge for the service is clear. The unwary traveller may be unpleasantly surprised how much porters will demand for their seemingly obliging assistance.

Passengers who cross either of the Bosphorus bridges at any time should be aware that the driver will add the toll to his fare. This is a reasonable means of recovering his cost, so a small variation in the meter fare is to be expected.

Shopping district of Taksim. Istanbul is a shopper's paradise, but tourists must bargain and watch out for pickpockets.

TOILETS

Western toilets are now more common throughout Turkey, although visitors will almost certainly encounter an eastern toilet at some point, probably in bars, restaurants and the countryside. In these areas, women may find it more convenient to wear a skirt rather than pants.

Travel Tip: Visitors should carry a small box of tissues as toilet paper is not always available.

CRIME AND SAFETY

While Turkey is probably as safe as most European countries, street crime and pickpockets are common in the major tourist areas of Istanbul. Visitors should be particularly wary of approaches from strangers offering to change money, to take them to a 'really good bar' or offering food and drink—regardless of how genuine and friendly they may seem. It is not unknown for unwary tourists to be found drugged, robbed and left in an alley. Visitors should take the usual, sensible precautions, such as **not** pulling out large wads of money when shopping; **using** the hotel's safety deposit box for passports and large amounts of cash (put in an envelope first); **not** leaving attractive and expensive items (e.g. *iPods*, cameras, etc.) lying around or clearly visible in hotel rooms.

In the key tourist areas of Istanbul such as the Grand (or Covered) Bazaar or anywhere in the Sultanahmet district, shoppers must be very careful of their personal effects. Visitors should be wary of anyone brushing up against them—should this occur, a check of the wallet immediately afterwards is recommended.

On the battlefield itself, visitors should note that there are certain hazards inherent in wandering off the main paths. In some areas the scrubby bush can hide a sheer drop or mask an old tunnel or trench. It is also easy to become disoriented and even lost in the numerous gullies and ravines at Gallipoli, especially in the Anzac area. Walkers should take plenty of water and should not rely on mobile phones as coverage does not extend to the whole of the Peninsula. In addition, unexploded and unstable munitions are known to remain littered about and visitors must remain vigilant.

HEALTH AND HOSPITALS

No vaccinations are necessary for travel to Turkey. Turkey's private hospitals (*hastane*) are very good and usually have English-speaking medical staff, but they are also expensive and foreign patients will need to have travel insurance to pay for any medical treatment. Visitors should ask their hotel reception staff for the location of the nearest hospital, should it be required. Travellers who receive medical treatment will need to retain their receipts so as to claim on their insurance once they return to Australia. While the tap water is generally safe to drink, most people use bottled water and visitors are urged not to drink from town springs. Generally, the only incident of 'Turkey Tummy' the visitor is likely to experience will come from poorly cooked food. As a precaution, travellers are strongly advised to travel with some diarrhoea tablets or anti-diarrhoea medication.

Once on the Gallipoli battlefields, visitors should watch out for the numerous mangy stray dogs. Most seem friendly as they rely on tourists for scraps of food. However, rabies is alive and well in some areas of Turkey and visitors are urged to keep their distance.

Chemist shops are generally common (except in rural areas), clean, well-stocked and helpful; it is not uncommon to find that the chemist speaks English. There is usually a chemist open somewhere, even after hours, and visitors should look for a sign saying *Eczane*. Hotel staff can also provide assistance in locating the nearest chemist.

Turkey has magnificent mosques, but visitors should try to choose a hotel that is not too close, or they may be woken very early.

VISITING A MOSQUE

Five times a day the *müezzin* calls the faithful to prayer in the mosque. Before entering a mosque, Muslims wash themselves and remove their shoes. Foreign visitors should also remove their shoes, avoid visiting the mosque during prayer time and show the respect they would any other house of worship. Women should cover their heads and arms and not wear shorts or short skirts. Men should not wear shorts and may feel more comfortable in a long-sleeved shirt (in certain famous mosques, overalls are provided for those not suitably dressed).

Travel Tip: Visitors should try not to stay in a hotel that is very close to a mosque or they will risk being woken by the first call to the faithful (*müezzin*) every morning at sunrise.

TIPS ON LOCAL LAWS AND CUSTOMS

Western Turkey (Istanbul and the Gallipoli area) is surprisingly Western in its outlook; there are remarkably few obvious cultural differences and most Australians are made to feel very welcome. However, religion can be a sensitive subject, so travellers should show due respect when visiting mosques (see above). Most visitors find that the Turkish culture becomes more conservative the further east they travel. Women should consider dressing more conservatively in eastern districts as shorts and T-shirts are less acceptable outside the tourist areas.

Turkey has strict laws against the use, possession or trafficking of illegal drugs. Those convicted of any of these offences can expect to receive a heavy fine or a prison sentence of four to twenty-four years. The export of antiquities, including items from the Gallipoli battlefield, is prohibited and carries a prison sentence from five to ten years. Likewise, the taking of photographs near military or official installations is prohibited. Homosexuality is not illegal, but is not widely tolerated. Public displays of affection between same sex couples could result in prosecution for public order offences. It is an offence to insult the Turkish nation or the national flag, or to deface or tear up currency.

EMERGENCY CONTACT DETAILS

In Turkey, the nation-wide 24-hour hotline number for **police** is **155**. Foreigners may also contact the Tourist Police in Istanbul on 0212 527 4503, or call in at Yerebatan Caddesi 6, Sultanahment—across the road from the Basilica Cistern—during office hours. For an **ambulance** call **112**.

OTHER USEFUL NUMBERS IN TURKEY

Ambulance	112
Fire	110
Police	155
International directory enquiries	118
Local directory inquiries	115

WORKING HOURS

Government offices

Monday–Friday
8:30-12:30 & 13:30-17:30

Saturday–Sunday (closed)

Banks

Monday–Friday
8:30-12-00 & 13:30-17:00

Saturday–Sunday (closed)

Shops
Monday–Saturday
9:30-13:00 & 14:00-19:00

Sunday (closed)

Istanbul covered market:
Monday–Saturday 8:00-19:00

Sunday (closed)

During the summer months, the government offices and many other establishments in the Aegean and Mediterranean regions close in the afternoon.

TIME DIFFERENCE

Australian Eastern Standard Time (EST) is +8 hours from Turkey (+9 for daylight saving time)

AUSTRALIAN CONSULAR ASSISTANCE IN TURKEY

Australian Consulate
Kolin Hotel
Kepez 17100
Canakkale TURKEY
Ph. (90 286) 218 1721
Fax. (90 286) 218 1724

Australian Embassy
88 Ugur Mumcu Caddesi
Gaziosmanpasa
Ankara TURKEY
Ph. (90 312) 459 9500
Fax. (90 312) 446 4827

Australian Consulate-General
2nd Floor, Suzer Plaza,
Askerocagi Caddesi No. 15,
Elmadag
Istanbul TURKEY
Ph. (90 212) 243 1333
Fax (90 212) 243 1332

SECTION 10: WHERE TO STAY

GALLIPOLI

Location. Early in the planning phase for a trip to Gallipoli, visitors should decide which town they will use as the accommodation base for their visit to the battlefields. This decision is likely to be based on personal preference, time of year and the duration of the visit and will ultimately come down to a choice between the eastern or western side of the Dardanelles. The west side (Eceabat and Kilitbahir) have the advantage of being closer to the battlefields. The east side (Çanakkale) will see visitors crossing by ferry each day, but provides easy access to shops and a wider assortment of bars, restaurants and hotels. Çanakkale, the largest town in the region, is also closer to the ruins of Troy, which is now a popular half-day trip for Aussie and Kiwi tourists. Visitors who are staying in the area for more than two days or who are travelling on to Izmir or other towns to the east should make Çanakkale their base. Those who are short on time, staying only overnight or who are returning to Istanbul or other towns to the north or north-west of the Dardanelles are better served by staying in Eceabat or Kilitbahir. Travellers with their own transport also have the option of staying closer to the battlefields.

Standard of accommodation. Visitors will also need to decide on the standard of accommodation that best suits their needs—from budget to more luxurious. This section includes a list of recommended hotels / hostels by area with an indication of their respective costs and facilities. Visitors should note that the entire area is usually booked out for Anzac Day each year, and that between March and September, Eceabat and Çanakkale are popular weekend holiday destinations for residents of Istanbul. Thus, a mid-week visit to the area will often present the best choice of hotel.

Holidays / celebrations. The main celebration in the Çanakkale region occurs on 18 March. This is Turkish Victory Day (*Çanakkale Deniz Zaferi*) and celebrates the Turkish defeat of the Allied navies attempting to force open the Dardanelles in 1915. While Anzac Day (25 April) is not specifically celebrated by the Turks, the entire Gallipoli Peninsula area is awash with thousands of Australian and New Zealand visitors at this time and local stallholders are out in force to cash in, adding to the appearance of a massive festival.

Çanakkale has the broadest range of accommodation in the Gallipoli area, but visitors should book early.
Opposite page: Çanakkale street map. *(Image by Mark Wahlert)*

ÇANAKKALE

Çanakkale (population 70,000) is the region's major town, tourist centre and transport hub. It sits on the famous Dardanelles which links the Mediterranean and Aegean seas to the Mamara and Black seas. The town's name reflects both its peacetime and military history: in years past Çanakkale was an important centre for Turkish pottery (*çanak* means 'pot') and has served as an important fortress (*kale*) to protect the narrowest section of the Dardanelles. The ancient city of Troy is only a short drive from Çanakkale. A picturesque town, Çanakkale is well served by restaurants, shops, museums and transport and is an excellent choice as a tourist base for touring the Gallipoli battlefields.

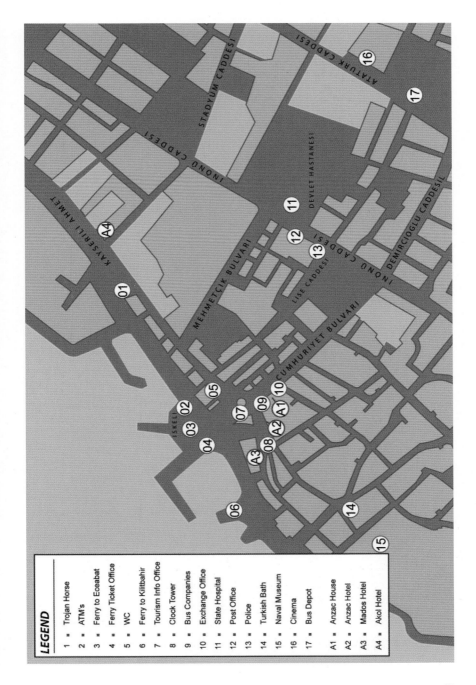

LEGEND

1 = Trojan Horse
2 = ATM's
3 = Ferry to Eceabat
4 = Ferry Ticket Office
5 = WC
6 = Ferry to Kilitbahir
7 = Tourism Info Office
8 = Clock Tower
9 = Bus Companies
10 = Exchange Office
11 = State Hospital
12 = Post Office
13 = Police
14 = Turkish Bath
15 = Naval Museum
16 = Cinema
17 = Bus Depot

A1 = Anzac House
A2 = Anzac Hotel
A3 = Mados Hotel
A4 = Akol Hotel

HOTELS IN ÇANAKKALE

Anzac House (A1) ★

Cumhuriyet Meydani No. 61.
Ph +90 286 213 59 69
www.anzachouse.com, Dbl-20YTL/pp,
Sgl-25YTL/pp, Triple/Quad-18YTL/pp,
Dorm-15YTL/pp.

This hotel is in a good location, only 100 metres from main ferry and bus terminal and close to shops and restaurants. The rooms are basic and small (some without windows) with shared bathroom facilities. There is a common room on the bottom floor with a small café. The rooms are key locked and there is a safety deposit box at reception. The hotel is tidy and clean and in a good state of repair. While it does not have a bar, there is an area for snacks and drinks (including alcohol). The staff speak good English and are friendly and helpful. The hotel has two shared internet terminals and caters specifically for Australians and New Zealanders. Hotel staff can arrange bus transfers to and from Istanbul and to and from Ephesus. The hotel doubles as an efficient tour agency, *Hassle Free Tours*, with daily (half-day) tours to Gallipoli and Troy. It is open 24 hours.

Anzac House.

Anzac Hotel (A2) ★ ★

Saat Kulesi Meydani No.8 – Clock
Tower Square. No. 12.
Ph +90 286 217 7777
www.anzachotel.com, Dbl-€38, Sgl-€28
Tariff only available in Euro.

This hotel is in a good location close to the ferry and bus terminal, shops and restaurants. Its rooms are average in size and include television, air conditioning and heating, ensuites and standard hotel amenities, but walls are very thin. The rooms are locked and opened with a pass and there is a safety deposit box at reception. The hotel is clean and tidy with both a bar and restaurant. The staff speak English and are friendly and helpful. Wireless internet is available. As the name suggests, the hotel caters specifically for Australians and New Zealanders with daily tours arranged to Gallipoli and Troy. Other tours and transport can also be organised and the hotel is open 24 hours.

Anzac Hotel.

Maydos Hotel (A3) ★ ★ ★

Yali Caddesi No. 12.
Ph +90 286 217 4090
www.maydos.com.tr Dbl-60YTL/pp,
Sgl-70YTL/pp, Triple-65YTL/pp,
40YTL/pp for room with no view.

This hotel boasts a great location on the water's edge, close to the ferry and bus terminal, shops and restaurants.

Its rooms are small to average sized, with television, air conditioning and heating, ensuites and standard hotel amenities. Some rooms have a view of the Dardanelles and all are locked and opened with a pass. There is a safety deposit box at reception. This is a clean, tidy and relatively new hotel with both a bar and restaurant on the lower level. The staff speak English and are friendly and helpful. Each room contains an ADSL port. Daily tours can be arranged to Gallipoli and Troy and bus transfers to and from Istanbul and to and from Ephesus are also on offer. The hotel operates the Maydos Restaurant on the water's edge at Eceabat. The hotel itself is open 24 hours.

Maydos Hotel.

Akol Hotel (A4) ★ ★ ★ ★

Kordonboyu 17100.
Ph +90 286 217 9456
www.hotelakol.com.tr Dbl-85YTL
average. Prices fluctuate depending on
season and occupancy rates. Check first.

The Akol Hotel is located about 400 metres from the ferry and bus terminal, opposite the water. It is close to shops and restaurants and features average-sized rooms, television, air conditioning, heating, ensuites and standard hotel amenities. Some floors are slightly run down, while others have been recently renovated. The rooms are locked and opened with a key pass and the hotel is equipped with security cameras. There are safety deposit boxes at reception and the hotel is generally clean and tidy. The Akol has a restaurant and bar, but both are expensive. Some staff speak English and are generally helpful. This hotel does not specifically cater for English-speaking patrons and there is no internet access. The bar includes a free pool table, but patrons are expected to drink as they play. The hotel is open 24 hours.

Kolin Hotel ★ ★ ★ ★ ★

Kepez 17100. Ph +90 286 218 0808
www.kolinhotel.com Dbl-170YTL average.

The Kolin Hotel is a ten-minute taxi ride from the ferry and bus terminal. It features good-sized rooms, television, air conditioning and heating, ensuites and above-average hotel amenities for this area. The hotel is spotless and well maintained. The rooms are locked and opened with a key pass and the hotel is equipped with security cameras. Each room contains a safe and a minibar. The hotel has a bar and restaurant, but both are expensive. There is usually at least one English-speaking staff member on duty and the staff, in general, are very helpful. The hotel has internet access. While the Kolin is not easy walking distance from the centre of town, it boasts excellent facilities including indoor and outdoor swimming pool, beach, pool, tennis court, bicycle course, walking course, barber and hair dresser, and more.

Akol Hotel.

ECEABAT

Eceabat (population 4,500) lies directly opposite Çanakkale's town centre on the opposite side of the Dardanelles. It is a pleasant, sleepy village which services the region's farming community and tourists visiting the Gallipoli battlefields. During the campaign Eceabat was known as Maidos and served as a Turkish headquarters and an important port for supplies. The town was devastated by Allied naval bombardments. Eceabat is 16 kilometres from Anzac Cove.

HOTELS IN ECEABAT

TJ's Hostel/Eceabat Hotel ★

Kemalpasa Mah. Cumhuriyet Cad. No. 5/A. Eceabat/C. Kale 17900 Phone +90.286.8143121 Fax +90.286.8143122 www. anzacgallipolitours.com Hostel prices: Dbl- €13/pp, Sgl- €18/pp, Dorm €10/ pp www.anzacgallipolitours.com Hotel prices: Dbl- €27/pp, Sg-l €35/pp.

This hostel/hotel is located in Eceabat close to the ferry and buses, and a limited number of shops and cafés. It features standard hostel and hotel rooms, all with private bathrooms. The hotel rooms have internet connection and air conditioning. The rooms are key-locked and there is a safety deposit box at reception. The hotel is tidy and clean and in good state of repair as it

is reasonably new. It boasts a roof bar, the staff speak good English and are friendly and helpful. A shared internet terminal is available. The hotel is run by an Australian-Turkish couple and caters specifically for Australians and New Zealanders, offering daily tours to Gallipoli and Troy (both tours are very good). Scuba diving and snorkelling tours of wrecks are also available. Private, group and trekking tours are available on request. Staff will help organise tours and transport for Gallipoli and for the rest of Turkey if required. One floor of the hotel houses the hostel, the other two comprise the hotel.

TJ's Hotel.

ACCOMMODATION NEAR THE BATTLEFIELDS

Camping – Kum Motel. Some visitors prefer to stay close to the battlefields so as to avoid the daily ferry trip from Çanakkale or the drive from Eceabat. The closest camping ground to the battlefields is the Kum Motel and Camping facility (*Kumkamp*),

about four kilometres south of the Kabatepe Information Centre and seven kilometres from Anzac Cove. It is a large camping area, close to beach and restaurant.
Tel: +90 286 814 14 55
begin_of_the_skype_highlighting
Fax: +90 286 814 26 65
begin_of_the_skype_highlighting
Email: rezervasyon@hotelkum.com, www.hotelkum.com

Hotel - Gallipoli Houses. A good hotel / cabin option close to Anzac Cove is the Gallipoli Houses. One of the newest hotels on the Peninsula, Gallipoli Houses offers comfortable, reasonably priced and convenient accommodation. The owners and managers, couple Eric and Özlem, are friendly and excellent hosts; always willing to assist. Prices are Dbl-€90 / pp, Sgl-€70, which includes breakfast and dinner. Kocadere Village, 17900 Eceabat / Çanakkale,
Tel : + 90 286 814 26 50 Fax : + 90 286 814 16 17 Email: talk2us@ gallipoli.com.tr, www.gallipoli.com. tr/accommodation_canakkale_hotels.htm

Gallipoli Houses.

ISTANBUL

Location. There are two main areas of central Istanbul that contain ideal accommodation for tourists: Beyoğlu and Sultanahmet. Beyoğlu is the main business and shopping district in Istanbul, while Sultanahmet is the principal tourist district. Both have excellent tourist facilities, including bars, clubs, entertainment and restaurants. Those visitors planning a short stay (two or three nights) should opt to stay in Sultanahmet as this is where most of the key tourist sites are located, many within a short walk of one another. However, those tourists planning to stay a week or more may prefer the Beyoğlu district, from which they can travel into Sultanahmet. Either way, visitors will probably find themselves spending some time in taxis commuting between the two districts.

Standard of accommodation. As for any large city, Istanbul offers a full range of accommodation. For those who prefer a budget-priced backpacker hotel, Sultanahmet provides the widest variety. However, for others who would prefer more luxurious accommodation, Beyoğlu is probably the best bet.

Cost of accommodation. Istanbul hotels seem to change their room tariffs almost hourly, depending on season, holidays or how busy they are (less so with the hotels at the upper end of the market as they charge such high prices that they are unaffected by variations in tourist numbers). The prices listed below, therefore, are only a guide. Visitors will need to check with their travel agent while planning their trip and ask for an acknowledgement from the Istanbul hotel, preferably on hotel letterhead or from the hotel e-mail account (visitors should bring this confirmation with them). Most hotels will display their room tariff on a board at reception, usually in US$ or €. Visitors should be aware that they do not necessarily have to pay this price. Everything in Istanbul can be negotiated.

Holidays / celebrations. A list of national holidays is included in Section 7. During these periods, the queues and traffic that plague Istanbul are likely to be worse than usual. Those who can avoid visiting Istanbul during these periods are well advised to do so. It pays to check websites such as *www.turkeytravelplanner.com/Religion/ramazan.html* for the dates of religious festivals such as *Ramazan* and *Kurban Bayrami*. These festivals are celebrated according to the Muslim lunar calendar and thus fall on different dates each year.

HOTELS IN BEYOĞLU/TAKSIM

Hotel Avrupa ★ ★

Topçu Caddesi 30, Talimhane, Taksim Ph +90 212 250 9420 Sgl 35-45YTL Dbl 45-60YTL.

This hotel features basic, but clean and comfortable rooms in bright colours. Some rooms also have ensuites. The hotel is in a good location and is a short walk to restaurants and the various night-time attractions. The hotel has a breakfast room but no bar. A cocker spaniel and a rabbit appear to run the reception area.

Hotel Residence ★ ★ ★

Sadi Ahşik Sokak 19, Beyoğlu Ph +90 212 252 7685 www.cantur.com.tr Sgl-45YTL, Dbl 65-75YTL.

The Hotel Residence is 25 kilometres from the Atatürk International Airport and well situated among the bars and nightlife of the Beyoğlu district. Those looking for a reasonably priced, clean hotel in a convenient location will find this hotel a good choice. Visitors should note, however, that the Hotel Residence can be hard to find. It is tucked away off a larger street—*Istiklal Caddesi.*

Cartoon Hotel ★ ★ ★

Tarlabaşı bulv. No. 36, Taksim
Ph +90 212 238 9328
www.cartoonhotel.com
Sgl €85 Dbl €95.

The Cartoon Hotel is directly opposite Taksim Square and close to the main shopping and entertainment area of Taksim, and the metro, funicular and bus terminals. While there is no pool, the hotel has a good rooftop lounge with views over Istanbul. It boasts friendly, helpful staff and clean rooms. If the hotel is not full, visitors should ask for a larger room with views (staff will initially offer a small room at the back of the hotel).

The Mamara Istanbul ★ ★ ★ ★ ★

Taksim Meydanı, Taksim
Ph +90 212 251 4696
www.themarmarahotels.com
Dbl 300-400YTL.

The Mamara is in an excellent location in the heart of Taksim Square with many rooms overlooking Taksim itself. It is a short walk to all the key shops, galleries, bars and the nightlife of Beyoğlu. The hotel is also close to the historic Dolmabahçe Palace and the Bosphorus. As with any international class five-star hotel, the facilities and service at the Mamara are superb. Those visitors who choose not to stay at this hotel should still try the fabulous ground floor café or the first floor Aqua Lounge bar to see first-hand what the beautiful people in Istanbul do to relax.

HOTELS IN SULTANAHMET

Orient Hostel ★

Akbiyik Cad 13, Sultanahmet
Ph +90 212 517 9493
www.orienthostel.com Dorm 20YTL,
Sgl 45YTL, Dbl 55YTL.

The Orient is a well-known backpacker hotel in a backpacker area of Sultanahmet. It boasts all the usual services (or lack of) expected of a backpacker, including café, bar and internet (including WiFi) access. The hostel is in a good location right next to the Topkapi Palace, and close to all the 'must see' sights. The rooms are clean and some include ensuites. The on-site travel service can arrange tours and transfers.

Best Western Hotel St Sophia ★ ★ ★

Alemdar Cad. No. 2, Sultanahmet
Ph +90 212 528 0973
www.bestwestern.com, Room tariff
varies with season, but averages
75-90YTL pp.

Renovated about ten years ago, this hotel was formerly an Ottoman Mansion. It is in a superb location next to the St Sophia Museum and only a few minutes' walk from the Blue Mosque, the Underground Cistern,

Topkapi Palace and the Grand Bazaar. There is a tram stop right outside the hotel's front door. The front desk staff speak English and are very friendly and helpful.

Four Seasons ★ ★ ★ ★ ★

Tevkifhane Sokak, Sultanahmet
Ph +90.212.638 8200
www.fourseasons.com,
Dbl 350-600YTL, Sgl 300-600YTL.

This is a deluxe hotel and arguably the best in Sultanahmet. Interestingly, it is a converted prison with only sixty-five rooms, but boasts excellent service, facilities and location.

TIPPING IN HOTELS

As a general rule, the more expensive and exclusive the hotel, the more prolific and expected tipping will be. For most establishments, however, it is usual to tip the porter about one YTL per bag that he carries to the room. Those visitors who have a car will ensure speedy service in garaging the car by passing the porter a one or two YTL tip.

SECTION 11: WHAT TO DO IN ISTANBUL

GETTING AROUND

Taxis and ferries. Taxis are easy to find and can be hailed just about anywhere in Istanbul. To compensate for language difficulties, visitors should keep a brochure or card from their hotel to show the driver. Similarly, those who plan to take a cab to a particular tourist attraction should ask hotel staff to write down their precise destinations so that these details can be shown to the driver (see also the guidelines on using cabs in Istanbul in Section 9). As Istanbul is really two cities, one on either side of the Bosphorus, ferries are common, cheap and enjoyable. There are regular services along the Bosphorus to key tourist sites such as the Golden Horn, Princes' Islands and Haydarpasa.

SIGHTSEEING

Visitors should plan their sightseeing by first collecting one of the many free tourist maps which will help guide them through their tour of the sights. Most hotels have copies of these maps; otherwise visitors can pick one up from the Tourist Information Office north-west of Sultanahmet Square (between Hagia Sophia and the Blue Mosque). Most of the key tourist sites are within walking distance of

Topkapi Palace.

this Tourist Information Office. For those visitors who are short of time, the key sites are listed here in order of proximity for easy visiting. Ultimately, however, the order of visiting will be simply a matter of personal preference.

Most tourist sites charge an entrance fee. Where possible, I have used AS$ for consistency as often the prices are quoted in YTL, € or US$. Use this price as a guide as prices change without notice. While the opening times for these sites were correct at time of printing, some may vary depending on the season. Visitors should check with hotel staff prior to their departure on a sightseeing jaunt.

A note of caution: pickpockets and bag snatchers do operate around these tourist sites. Sightseers should keep an eye and a tight grip on their valuables at all times.

> *Travel Tip:* Navigating the narrow sidestreets of Sultanahmet, especially in the bazaar district, can be extremely difficult. To assist in locating the various sites, I have included the local name along with the tourist name for each of these sites. Visitors should either carry this book with them on their walk or write down the local names to assist in asking directions from the local people who, while few of them speak English, are generally very friendly.

Topkapi Palace (*Topkapi Sarayi*). *Open 9.00 a.m.–5.00 p.m. Wed–Mon, entry AS$20.* Conveniently situated close to Aya Sofia and other tourist sites in Sultanahmet, Topkapi Palace was home to Turkey's sultans for four centuries. This 500-year-old palace is an enthralling complex in which to wander. There are magnificent views of the Bosphorus, several intriguing museums and collections of Ottoman weapons, armour, treasures and jewellery. Many of the sacred relics of Islam were brought to the palace after the conquest of Egypt in the sixteenth century and have been preserved here ever since. Items now on display include the swords and bow of Mohammed, his mantle (cloak) and hairs from his beard, along with bones from John the Baptist.

Hagia Aya (Saint) Sophia (*Aya Sofya Meydani*). *Open 9.00 a.m.–5.00 p.m. Tues– Sun, entry AS$20.* Arguably Istanbul's most famous monument, Hagia Sophia was built as a Roman Church in the sixth century, converted to a mosque in the fifteenth century, and redesigned as a museum in 1935. Nothing was spared in building this magnificent church, one of the finest examples in the world. Over ten thousand craftsmen worked on the construction which was completed in fewer than six years—an amazing achievement for the time. The church is decorated with a variety of fascinating mosaics, each one boasting its own unique historical significance.

Hagia Sophia.

Basilica Cistern (*Yerebatan Sarniçi*). *Open every day 9.30 a.m.–5.30 p.m., entry AS$10.* Visitors exiting Hagia Sophia into Sultanahmet Square will notice a small building to the north-west (on *Yerebatan Cad*). This is the entry point for a view of the largest and most magnificent covered cistern (water storage) in the city. The cistern, one of a number in the old city, was built by the Greeks in the sixth century and fed via a Roman aqueduct that carried water 19 kilometres from the northern countryside (remnants of these aqueducts can still be seen throughout Istanbul). This cathedral-sized, cavernous underground water tank has 336 columns, many of which are intricately decorated, can hold 80,000 cubic metres of water and was used as a location for the 1963 James

Bond film *From Russia with Love*. Visitors can enjoy a coffee and the great atmosphere and acoustics in the little café.

Sultanahmet (Blue) Mosque (*Sultan Ahmet Camii*). *Open 9.00 a.m.–7.00 p.m. daily, entry by donation.* A key Istanbul landmark, this seventeenth-century mosque is famous for its beautiful blue tile work and breathtaking interiors. As this mosque is still used by the faithful, visitors should be conscious of prayer times as the mosque will be closed to tourists. To avoid disappointment, visitors should arrange a morning visit or take an organised tour.

Decorative ceiling of the Blue Mosque.

Hippodrome (*Atmeydani*). *Open all hours, free entry.* On the north-western side of the Blue Mosque on Meydani Sk., is the site of the old Hippodrome. Built by Roman Emperor Septimus Severus in the second century, the Hippodrome became the centre of social life in Roman and Byzantine Istanbul. Not only were the more traditional chariot and horse races held here, but the Hippodrome also served a similar role to the Roman Colosseum and staged bloody gladiatorial combat, fights between men and wild animals, and mock naval battles. Some of the original monuments that adorned the Hippodrome remain today: the Egyptian Obelisk, the Serpent Column and the Walled Obelisk. The Egyptian Obelisk is the oldest monument in Istanbul and dates back to 1490 BC when the Egyptian Pharaoh Thutmose III erected it before his temple at Luxor. It was transported to, and erected at, the Hippodrome with great difficulty in the fourth century AD.

Grand Bazaar (*Kapali Çarsi* or covered market). *Open 8.30 a.m.–7.00 p.m. Mon-Sat, entry free.* A trip to the Grand Bazaar is a must for anyone visiting Istanbul. There are literally thousands of shops (over 3,000) selling just about everything: Turkish carpets, leather goods, copies of famous clothing brands, pottery, etc, etc, etc. There are also numerous cafés and a restaurant to provide an opportunity to escape the shoppers and traders, although it is a more expensive to eat in the bazaar than in the adjoining streets. Visitors should keep track of their progress through the bazaar, as it is very easy to become lost in the myriad of over 60 streets and laneways. Most shoppers are amazed at the talented and unique ways that the merchants will use to try to entice them into their shops. One is reputed to use a priceless piece of Aussie slang by yelling at passing Australians, 'Jeez mate, some bastard's stolen me f***in' ute!'

Travel Tip: Shoppers should be aware that they will need to bargain in the Grand Bazaar as few shops display prices (see Section 12). Tourists who venture out of the covered market into the surrounding sidestreets will most likely be 'set upon' by hordes of boys selling a variety of wares. These are seasoned operators who are not put off by a simple 'No!' It is best to ignore these young vendors and walk straight ahead.

Spice Bazaar (*Mısır Çarşısı* or Egyptian Bazaar). *Open 8.30 a.m.–6.30 p.m. Mon–Sat, entry free.* Having left the Grand Bazaar, visitors should walk downhill along *Uzunçarsi Caddesi* (Longmarket Street) to the Spice Bazaar and treat themselves to some of the most mouth-watering delicacies Istanbul has to offer. Those who become lost in the maze of narrow streets should simply head north towards the Golden Horn or the Galata Bridge and they will come across the district that houses the Spice Bazaar. Visitors should try the stuffed figs or chocolate-coated dates. Jewellery stores and other merchants can also be found nearby. This is truly an amazing place and well worth a visit—even just a stroll between the Spice and Grand Bazaars will provide a glimpse of the daily life of old Istanbul.

Travel Tip: Purchasing the attractive boxes of Turkish Delight found in the bazaars is not recommended. Shoppers who bring these home will find that they are half empty and only contain the cheapest of ingredients. Instead, Turkish Delight can be bought in bulk from one of the stallholders in the Spice Bazaar. This way, the purchaser will know precisely what is being bought and can also choose a variety not available in the pre-packed samples. The shop keeper will usually vacuum seal the package for you.

Mosque of Süleiman the Magnificent (*Suleymaniye Camii*). *Open 9.00 a.m.– 7.00 p.m. daily, entry free.* Located in Sultanahmet due west of the Spice Market and off *Prof. Siddik Sami Onar Caddesi*, this mosque is one of

the 'must see' sights of Istanbul. It is a magnificent example of early Ottoman architecture, having been built in the sixteenth century for one of the most famous sultans, Sultan Süleiman the Magnificent. The four great minarets surrounding the entrance courtyard are said to signify that Süleiman was the fourth sultan to rule in Istanbul. Visitors entering the courtyard are immediately struck by the size of the dome which measures 53 metres high and 27.25 metres across. Also spectacular are the wonderful stained glass windows that capture the sunlight in an amazing array of colour.

Military Museum (*Askeri Müzesi*). *Open 9.00 a.m.–5.00 p.m. Wed– Sun, entry A$5, or A$12 including permission to take photographs.* The Military Museum is located at Harbiye, approximately one kilometre north of Taksim Square. Even for those who do not consider themselves military buffs, this museum is worth the trip. There are 22 rooms housing an impressive list of about 9,000 items. Some superb examples of Ottoman weapons, armour and other militaria are on show. The upper floor houses an excellent display dedicated to the Gallipoli campaign—worth seeing if only to gain a Turkish military perspective. The *Mehter*, the world's oldest military band, plays each afternoon at 3.00 p.m. and 4.00 p.m.

EATING AND RELAXING

Istanbul Military Museum. The *Mehter*, the world's oldest military band, plays each afternoon.

Galata Tower *(Galata Kulesi). Open 9.00 a.m.–8.00 p.m. every day, entry AS$15.* Located on the northern side of Galata Bridge (an easy walk from Sultanahmet), the Galata Tower was originally built as a lighthouse in 527 AD. While it has been rebuilt and renovated many times, its appearance today reflects its seventeenth-century façade. The Tower provides magnificent views across Istanbul and visitors can lunch in the restaurant between midday and 4.00 p.m.

Galata Tower offers magnificent views over Istanbul and the Bosphorus.

Eating areas. Regardless of whether visitors stay in Sultanahmet, Taksim or Beyoğlu, good eating places abound, from the relatively cheap cafés to the more exclusive and expensive restaurants. Turkey has remarkably good food and it is usually enjoyed at a slow pace; the Western concept of fast food has not as yet made major inroads in Turkey. While visitors are unlikely to find English spoken in Turkish restaurants, those that cater for tourists usually have either an English menu or a menu in Turkish with pictures of the various meals available. Typical Turkish meals familiar to most Australians include *köfte* (meat balls), *kebaps* (kebabs or roast meats), *pide* (pizza) and *çorbe* (soup). These dishes are usually served with vegetables, salads, large quantities of bread and gallons of *çay* (tea). Vegetarians should try *meze* (stuffed vegetables). Diners who are after something quick and cheap should try the Turkish pizza (*pide*), which can come with a variety of toppings, or a *Döner kebap*, available almost everywhere and usually served in an envelope of *pide* bread.

> ***Travel Tip:*** Be wary of eating places that do not display their prices. This may mean that these will be more expensive than most foreign diners expect. Always ask the price BEFORE ordering.

Turkish bath (*hamam*). The Turkish bath is an ancient tradition that merged with that of the Roman bath in the Byzantine period. In earlier times the Turkish bath was more a luxury enjoyed by the wealthy and high born. With the arrival of Islam, however, and the Muslim's reverence for cleanliness, the Turkish bath took on new meaning for all. More than just a place to bathe, the bathhouses have become social centres for both sexes and an integral part of Turkish culture.

Cabaret (including belly dancing). Like the Turkish bath, belly dancing is very popular in Turkey. Dancers are admired for their ability to *göbek atmak* (toss the belly-button), which requires extremely well developed abdominal muscles. Small finger cymbals, called *zil*, are used by the dancers to accompany their moves. The dancers move very close and even dance in and amongst the audience. This is because it is usual for appreciative observers to place bank notes into the dancer's flimsy clothing. There are numerous nightclubs in Istanbul where tourists can watch a belly dancing show. Hotel staff can recommend a cabaret, or visitors can take one of the many organised tours that include this form of entertainment.

Take in a movie. While the sights of Istanbul are magnificent, many visitors find the need to rest from sightseeing and just relax for an afternoon and take in a movie. The cinemas in Istanbul are generally very good; western films are most usually in English and visitors may see a movie several months before its is released in Australia (Turkey is privy to the European releases). Prices are a little cheaper than in Australia and Turkish cinemas still have ushers and lolly-boys.

Internet access. While some hotels do provide internet access, this service is certainly not cheap, particularly in the more expensive hotels. In backpacker accommodation, there are usually only one or two terminals to service all guests. Some of the more modern or recently refurbished hotels are installing WiFi. Generally there is no shortage of internet access as internet cafés are very popular in Turkey and are extremely cheap (a few YTL an hour). In most of these cafés patrons can not only keep in touch with friends and family in Australia, but also play a wide variety of games (solo or networked), order drinks (hot or cold) and some cafés even provide light meals. In Istanbul, internet cafés are most prolific in the tourist areas of Sultanahmet, but can also be found down some of the many sidestreets in Taksim and elsewhere.

SECTION 12: BARGAINING

While bargaining is a way of life in Turkey, it is a custom that often leaves Australians and New Zealanders feeling uncomfortable. However, Turkish merchants expect shoppers to bargain and it can be fun. Visitors who would like to try their hand at bargaining should follow these simple steps:

Know what you want. Be clear in your own mind exactly what it is you want—the colour, size, make, etc. It is easy to be distracted by an experienced merchant who may try to confuse you with various options and then try to convince you to purchase a particular item. If it is not what you want **do not buy it**!

Know what the going price is. Do not buy from the first shop you walk into, regardless of what a great deal you seem to be getting. Shop around to see what the item you want is selling for, how many there are, what choice there may be, etc. One option is to chat with other tourists about what they bought and what they paid.

Know your bottom line. Do your homework before you leave Australia and know what an equivalent item would be worth at home. Note, however, that in Turkey it is likely to be a copy, rather than an original,

and this should be factored into your bargaining. Having looked around the local shops, get a feel for what you think a fair price would be, establish your 'bottom line' and stick to it.

Don't appear keen. When you have decided what it is you want, and the price you want to pay, start to casually ask for a price from a merchant. When you do this, do not appear too enthusiastic. The merchant will be trying to establish how high he should set his opening price. If you appear keen he is likely to try a high price. If, however, he feels you are not so eager he may not want to scare you off. Treat this as a game and play your role. You can have fun doing it and you will be surprised how successful you can be.

Bargaining can be fun provided you play the game. Being timid will just mean that you will pay too much.

The counter-offer. Force the merchant to give you a price. Often he will ask you what you are prepared to pay. Force him to play your game; do not play by his rules. Continue to ask for a price (remembering not to appear too keen). The price you will be given will initially be a long way above what the merchant expects you to pay (but he can always hope). Now comes the difficult question—what do you bid in your counter-offer? There is no clear answer to this. Some may advise to just halve the initial price, or even offer a quarter, but this does not take into account your specific situation and might just serve to prove that you are a novice at bargaining. It is better to keep in mind what you think is a fair price, what you would pay at home, whether the item is a fake, how common the item is in the area you are shopping (the merchant will know if you can simply go next door and buy it more cheaply) and what the other merchants are trying to sell it for. Come back with a counter-offer that is less than what you are prepared to pay (the merchant will try and negotiate it up), but not so low that the merchant simply refuses to negotiate further.

Walking Away. When you reach your 'bottom line' do not move on it. If necessary, just thank the merchant and walk out of his shop. You will soon know if your price is close to what the merchant will accept. He will either let you depart (which should give you a good idea what his bottom line is and you can return later with another price), or make an even better offer. It is not unusual to see several shoppers wandering around the markets in Turkey with one or two merchants at their heels continuing to haggle. Conversely, do not feel obliged to buy the item because of the time the merchant has spent with you. It is usual for you to be offered a hot or cold drink and snacks, and for the merchant to spend some time showing you his wares. However, you are under no obligation to buy.

Closing the deal. Do not offer a price if you are not prepared to honour it. Once you state a price you have entered into a verbal contract. Unless you have negotiated another method of payment, you should pay in cash. Finally, do not continue bargaining over the last few cents. If you are close enough to your price, accept it and be happy with the deal, even if someone else later tells you they got the same thing for a little bit less.

SECTION 13: WHAT TO DO WHILE ON THE GALLIPOLI PENINSULA

TRAVEL AROUND GALLIPOLI

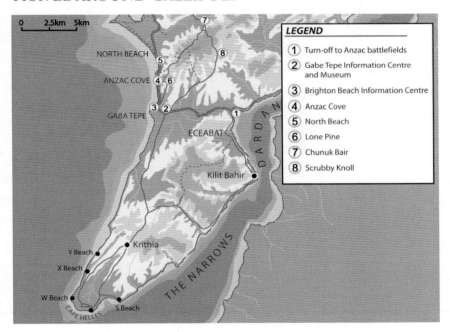

LEGEND

1. Turn-off to Anzac battlefields
2. Gabe Tepe Information Centre and Museum
3. Brighton Beach Information Centre
4. Anzac Cove
5. North Beach
6. Lone Pine
7. Chunuk Bair
8. Scrubby Knoll

Gallipoli road map.

Tourist office. There is a good tourist office next to the main ferry terminal at Çanakkale. Visitors can check here for local maps, guides and other information including 'what's on' in the Gallipoli area. There is usually a member of staff on duty who speaks English. The best place to obtain maps of the battlefields, however, is the Kabatepe War Museum. This museum has sole rights for all National Park maps that are produced.

Hitch-hiking/walking. The local people around the Gallipoli area are very friendly and will usually offer hitch-hikers a lift. In summer there is generally enough traffic for hitch-hikers to travel easily from Eceabat out to the Gabe Tepe Museum (about 13 kilometres) and back. Around the actual battlefield itself, however, traffic is minimal and those without pre-arranged transport will almost certainly have to walk. In winter there is also far less traffic, especially late in the afternoon, which may leave hitch-hikers facing a long, cold and wet walk home. For the fit and more adventurous, the Anzac battlefields offer some excellent walking trails. Walkers should be aware, however, that the area is very hilly and some of the trails between the coast and the inland ridges are goat tracks at best and downright dangerous at worst. It is best to allow two days to walk the entire area.

Travel Tip: Women are advised not to walk around the battlefields alone as there have been incidents of sexual assault in the more remote areas of the Peninsula. Many parts of the Anzac battlefield are very remote and isolated.

One of the best ways to see the Gallipoli battlefields is to get off the beaten track.

Taxis. Taxis can be difficult to find in the Gallipoli area, apart from around Çanakkale or the Eceabat ferry terminal. Visitors are advised to hire a taxi from Eceabat as it will save paying for the cab to take the ferry from Çanakkale. Passengers should note that, while most Çanakkale cabs use a meter, many in Eceabat do not, and the fare has to be negotiated. This is best accomplished through an interpreter who pre-negotiates a deal or by asking hotel staff to write down the precise details of the trip. Passengers can then use sign language to negotiate a price. The taxi drivers are certainly used to this. Those who use a taxi with a meter should ensure that **it is turned on** at the start of the journey. A two-to-three-hour taxi hire to travel the battlefield should cost around AS$60 to $80.

Travel Tip: There are a few taxi drivers in the area who speak reasonable English; however passengers should not rely on their commentary on the Gallipoli campaign as they are not qualified guides and few understand the battles that were fought.

Buses and Dolmus. Buses run on regular routes throughout the peninsula area—even out to Troy. Visitors keen to secure details of when they run and to where, should either visit the Otogar (bus deport) in

Çanakkale or the Tourist Information Office just next to the Çanakkale ferry dock. The Dolmus resembles a minivan that runs a set route, picking people up anywhere along its run until it is full. These are very cheap and cover a vast area. Information on how to use the Dolmus and what routes they follow can be obtained through hotel staff or a visit to the Çanakkale Tourist Information Office mentioned above. Note that using the Dolmus to travel out to the battlefields is not recommended as it may result in a long walk home.

Vehicle ferry between Çanakkale and Eceabat.

Ferries. There is a regular ferry service from Çanakkale to either Eceabat or Kilitbahir. The ferry to Eceabat departs on the hour every hour depending on the season. The ferry to Kilitbahir departs when it is full (about every thirty to forty-five minutes in summer). Visitors should check times at the ferry terminal in advance. The Çanakkale—Kilitbahir

service takes about fifteen minutes and costs approximately AS$15 for one car and two people, or AS$1.50 per person. Çanakkale to Eceabat takes about thirty minutes and costs around AS$20 for a car and two passengers, or AS$2 per person.

Travel Tip: The Eceabat service is the most convenient. However, visitors can take the ferry to Kilitbahir if they miss the ferry to Eceabat and would prefer not to wait.

Self-drive. The battlefield sites are about ten to twelve kilometres from the nearest towns of Çanakkale and Eceabat. While guided tours of the battlefield are available (see below), visitors may prefer to hire a self-drive car and wander the area at their leisure using this book as their guide. A self-drive car will allow the freedom to spend as much time on the battlefields as desired. The minimum period recommended for even a brief look over the battlefield is half a day to a whole day.

Guided tours. Several companies offer guided tours of the battlefield. These are ideal for those who are short of time (most last from three to five hours) and will provide a good overview of the campaign. However, the battlefields are extensive and group guided tours, while good value for money, often gloss over key aspects of the campaign and can provide inaccurate information. Information on tour options is readily available from the Tourist Office at the Çanakkale ferry terminal. Tour companies that I have used, and that provide a good service, include *TJ's* in Eceabat www.anzacgallipolitours.com and *Hassle Free Travel Agency* in Çanakkale www.anzachouse.com.

> ***Travel Tip:*** Visitors who take a TJ's daily tour and then stay on for a few days with TJ's in Eceabat will be treated to free transport out to the battlefield with the TJ's battlefield tour group for the duration of their stay. This is a popular option for many people who want to trek around Gallipoli as they can arrange a trail itinerary with the TJ's guide which also designates a pick-up point for the bus driver at the end of the day.

Car hire. Visitors who arrive in the area by bus can hire a car from one of the local rental companies. There are several companies in Çanakkale. One reliable company I use is *Gezgin Oto Rental.* This company's address: *Cumhuriyet Meydani Tekke Sk. No. 2/A. Phone: (286) 212 83 92).* Those visitors using a local hire car company must book early in peak periods.

FOOD

There is no shortage of cheap eats throughout the region, although fine dining restaurants can be difficult to find. As with everything else, food prices are sometimes higher over the Anzac Day period.

Eceabat. A short walk along the row of shops and bars fronting the ferry terminal will quickly highlight the culinary options. There are a few *pide* (Turkish pizza) and *kebap* cafés in this area that offer good food at a reasonable price. Those visitors looking for something more romantic or upmarket will find themselves with a rather limited choice in Eceabat. One of the better restaurants in town is at the Liman Hotel and has some of the best seafood in the region. A meal of *meze* (stuffed vegetables) in the pleasant outside garden overlooking the Dardanelles is also a culinary treat.

Boomerang Bar, the key location for a drink over the Anzac Day period in Eceabat.

Çanakkale. Like Eceabat, Çanakkale offers a quick, cheap feed at any one of the food stalls or cafés opposite the ferry terminal. Other restaurants and cafés dot the main street opposite the ferry / bus stop (*Cumhuriyet Bul*). Depending on the weather, more pleasant views are available at the numerous bars and cafés on the waterfront north of the ferry terminal. Many of Çanakkale's hotels now boast rooftop bars and restaurants. These are a mixed bag and I have found that street-level dining is difficult to surpass for variety and price. For an entirely different culinary experience, call in at *Köy Evi* at Yali Caddesi 13 (one of the sidestreets running south from the clock tower). This café is run by two women who make fabulous home-cooked country meals at very affordable prices. Try one of the numerous *kebap* houses for the Turkish equivalent of McDonald's.

The Çanakkale clocktower. A landmark in Çanakkale close to restaurants, internet cafes and hotels.

DRINK

Despite that fact that most Turks are Muslim, there is no shortage of bars in either Eceabat or Çanakkale. In both these towns, bars populate the water's edge in sight of the ferry terminal, with the more traditional coffee houses down the back streets. The local beer, *Efes*, is very good, but I would advise giving the local spirit, *raki,* a wide berth. Many of the cafés and restaurants sell both beer and local wine, except during *Ramazan*. The local wine, however, is something of an acquired taste. At those bars where there are no kitchen facilities, the staff will usually bring food in for visitors who have settled into an extended drinking session. It is not uncommon to see boys running between the bars with large plates of steaming *kofte, pide* or *kebaps.*

ENTERTAINMENT

Eceabat has a very limited range of evening entertainment. During busy periods, and especially during the Anzac Day week, the Boomerang Bar in Eceabat is one of the liveliest places around. An unlikely dive of a place, it serves cheap beer and is a known hangout for thirsty young Australians and New Zealanders. An alternative is one of the numerous bars and nightclubs in Çanakkale. Visitors should head for the clock tower near the ferry terminal, follow the noise, and remember to stay away from the *raki*.

Çanakkale also boasts a five-screen cinema about one kilometre east of the ferry terminal (near the main bus depot or *Otogar*). There will usually be at least one modern movie in English being screened, often a new release yet to be screened in Australia.

INTERNET ACCESS

As in Istanbul, internet cafés are very popular and easy to find. While the staff may not speak English, they are usually very friendly and sign language will often suffice. Almost every sidestreet around the centre of Çanakkale will have at least one internet café with high-speed access. Visitors travelling with a friend who are looking for more entertainment than Turkish television can provide should try a few networked games. Turkish internet cafés will have the latest games (often pirated copies) and visitors can enjoy a few hours for just a few YTL.

HEALTH

Çanakkale has an excellent private hospital with English-speaking staff. Visitors should ask their hotel's reception staff for the location of the nearest doctor or hospital (*hastane*).

Any receipts for medical treatment should be requested and retained to allow the lodging of an insurance claim once back in Australia.

MONEY

Çanakkale offers the best financial services with plenty of ATMs along the waterfront (north of the ferry terminal) and throughout the town. A new ATM is also located a few hundred metres down from the ferry terminal at Eceabat. There are several banks in Çanakkale which are located close to the ferry terminal or along the main road running east. They are open from 8.30 a.m. to 12.00 p.m., and from 1.30 p.m. to 5.00 p.m. Using a bank is not recommended as it is an incredibly tedious and time-consuming exercise. Those visitors who brave the bank bureaucracy must ensure that they bring their passport for identification. Most local hotels will cash travellers' cheques, although at a less favourable rate. The majority of hotels and restaurants in Çanakkale, and some in Eceabat, will take Euros, but also at a rate more favorable to them. Financial services in the rest of the region are sparse.

SECTION 14: THINGS TO TRY OUT

Local barber. Male visitors looking for a totally relaxing experience should try visiting a local barber. For the price of a standard cut in Australia or New Zealand, the local barber will wash hair, massage the scalp, perform an old-fashioned shave and cut the hair (including nasal and ear hair if requested). There are a few old-fashioned barbers in Eceabat and several in Çanakkale.

Turkish bath (*hamam*). There are a few good bath houses in Çanakkale. One I can certainly recommend for male visitors is Yeli Haman which is between the ferry terminal and the Military Museum (No. 14 on the Çanakkale street map). Note that times vary for men and women, so visitors should check first. The full routine should cost less than AS$30. A tip of around four to five YTL should be paid to the masseur/masseuse prior to the service. While the Yeli Haman also serves women, a better female bath house is the Çanakkale Hamam, which is just over the bridge from the Çanakkale Friday market area.

Souvenirs and Turkish carpets (*Kilim*). Local shops selling numerous (usually tacky) souvenirs abound on the waterfront at both Çanakkale and Eceabat. The Çanakkale area is well known for its fine carpets, or *kilim,* which come in all sizes and prices and the local vendor can arrange postage back to Australia and New Zealand. Purchasers should ensure, however, that there is no animal hair in the weave or the carpet may fall foul of Customs or the Australian Quarantine Inspection Service (AQIS). Cheap examples are available in the tourist shops near the ferry terminal, with the better stores only a short walk from the Clock Tower in Çanakkale. Hotel staff can provide directions.

REGIONAL SIGHTSEEING

Troy (*Troja*). The ancient city of Troy dates back to 3000 BC. Made famous by Homer's *The Iliad* and, more recently, the movie starring Brad Pitt, it is only a short drive (about 30 minutes or 15 kilometres) from Çanakkale. There are daily tours to Troy from many of the Çanakkale hotels. An organised tour (usually around half a day) is recommended, as Troy is, in fact, nine cities layered upon one another and a good guide can bring each layer alive for the visitor and even indicate the place where Achilles fought Hector. Visitors should try to avoid weekends as the site can become crowded with school children.

Troy theatre.

The fortress walls of Troy.

Replica Trojan Horse.

The plain where Achilles is said to have fought Hector.

Troy's wooden horse. The horse on display at the entrance to the Troy archaeological site is a tacky replica of the legendary Trojan horse. However this does not seem to deter tourists from climbing all over it to pose for a holiday snap. More impressive is the wooden horse used in Hollywood's 2004 movie, *Troy*, which can be seen in Morabbin Park, Çanakkale (along the waterfront north of the ferry terminal, opposite the Akol Hotel).

Military Museum and Çimenlik Castle. The Çimenlik Castle or fortress *(open 9.00 a.m.–noon and 1.30–5.00 p.m. Tue–Wed and Fri–Sun)* was originally constructed in the fifteenth century as part of the system of control along the Dardanelles Straits. The castle played a central role during the Allied naval attack on the Straits in 1915 and the damage caused by British and French warships can still be seen. The military museum inside contains militaria from the Ottoman period as well as World War I.

The Çanakkale Archeology Museum *(open 9.00 a.m.–5.00 p.m. Tue–Sun).* For those interested in ancient history, the five halls of the Çanakkale Museum contain a rich collection of artifacts unearthed from the various excavations in the region, including Troy.

Çanakkale's Trojan Horse.

Kilitbahir Fortress *(open 8.30 a.m.–noon, and 1.30–6.00 p.m. Wed–Sun).* Just a short ferry ride across the Straits from Çanakkale, the fortress at Kilitbahir is certainly worth a visit. Inside the fortress' stone walls is a fascinating collection of Ottoman militaria, behind the fortress itself is an interesting set of bunkers, and there are great views from the ramparts. Visitors should try some local coffee or tea from the seaside café at the foot of the castle.

Kilitbahir fortress.

Güzelyali. Summer on the Peninsula can be very hot and many visitors find themselves hankering for a place to swim, windsurf or snorkel. A short drive or taxi ride to the Güzelyali seaside (10 minutes or 12 kilometres from Çanakkale) will bring visitors to long sandy beaches swept by almost constant breezes. Local beachside vendors hire out a variety of water sport equipment.

Gulf of Saros. The Anzac battlefields are close to the southern shores of the Gulf of Saros, which contains numerous shipwrecks from the Gallipoli campaign. This makes the area a popular dive spot. Those keen to dive these wrecks should ask hotel staff to direct them to one of the local dive shops in Çanakkale.

Gökçeada Island. Gökçeada Island, lying about 23 kilometres from the mainland, is an interesting place for a day tour. The island (formerly known as Imros) was an important staging area for Allied troops fighting in the Peninsula, and served as General Hamilton's headquarters. Gökçeada Island contains numerous old Greek churches and even more monasteries, as well as many lovely lakes and waterfalls. This is a good day trip to take to escape the heat of the mainland in summer. Ferries for Gökçeada depart regularly from Kabatepe, although their schedule varies according to the season. Hotel staff or the Çanakkale Tourist Information Office can provide an accurate schedule for interested visitors.

> ***Travel Tip:*** It is a bit of a run from the ferry terminal at Gökçeada into town, and the taxi drivers will try to overcharge passengers. Visitors should ensure that they pre-negotiate a rate with the driver **before** getting into the cab.

SECTION 15: TAKING A CAR

The distance from the airport to Çanakkale is approximately 350 kilometres or between four to five hours' drive (depending on stops and traffic). Once out of Istanbul the road is generally good, traffic moderate and the journey quite pleasant. Drivers should note that Turkey has one of the highest road accident rates in the world and fatalities occur frequently. Caution should be exercised on all roads at all times, especially at night or on country roads. The Gallipoli Peninsula is located in a national park, with the additional hazards of farm machinery, animals, poor roads and an absence of signs and lighting.

For those intending to stay more than six months, an international driving licence is required, and is highly recommended as vehicle rental companies may require a translation of the renter's licence into Turkish. As in Australia, drink-driving is considered a serious offence. The police regularly breathalyse drivers, fine those over the limit on the spot (currently 340YTL) and will immediately confiscate the offender's licence. Vehicles are left-hand drive and, while this does not present a major difficulty, driving a left-hand drive car for the first time in

Istanbul traffic is not recommended. Turkish roads are generally sealed and in good condition, although in some areas of the Gallipoli Peninsula the road is pot-holed, dirt or gravel (which can be hazardous in wet or icy conditions). Visitors should plan to drive no more than 350 kilometres per day. This will allow adequate time for sightseeing and rest periods without the need to travel at night. An air-conditioned vehicle is a must in summer.

DIRECTIONS FROM THE AIRPORT (SELF-DRIVE)

Before you leave the car park, reset the car's odometer to '0' and use the distances below as a guide:

1. after you exit the airport security parking area, keep left and then, at the major roundabout, turn left and follow the signs to the motorway and EDIRNE

2. **10 km** - exit right onto Route E.80

3. **11 km** - toll gate. Enter 'Billet' lane and push green button to collect your ticket. Do not use the right-hand lane at the toll

booth as cars tend to stop illegally to drop people off or collect them, causing congestion.

4. **70 km** - after about 45 minutes of travelling, look out for the signs for the D.100 on the right, and the route to TEKIRDAG & IPSALA. Keep right as, at around 72 kilometres, you will enter the toll booth – toll is 2.25YTL.

5. **80 km** - D.100 veers right. Stay to the left and follow the main flow of traffic and signs to TEKIRDAG.

6. **87 km** - you should now start to see the Sea of Marmara. The road is now running parallel to the coast.

7. **130 km** - you should now be entering the outskirts of TEKIRDAG. Continue to follow the main road and the D.110, but keep an eye out for the first road sign to Çanakkale. Tekirdag is famous for Turkey's favourite drink, *raki*, brewed in a local factory, and for a special form of *köfte* (meat balls).

8. **140 km** - as you leave Tekirdag, stay on the D.110 and follow the sign to MALKARA and then KESAN

9. **142.5 km** - look for the large OPET petrol station on the right-hand side of the road. This is a good spot to stop for a break and celebrate 'surviving' Istanbul traffic. Full services are available. If you have not done so already, try the Turkish coffee (you need to order and pay for it at the cash register then hand your ticket over where the coffee is made).

10. **215 km** - turn left at the roundabout onto the E.90 and follow the signs to KESAN and GELIBOLU. As you leave Kesan, you will see the first sign for ÇANAKKALE. Follow that sign.

11. **240 km** - on the left and back from the road in a low, brown, wooden building is a restaurant that serves excellent food and has clean toilets. If you use the toilets, you will need some small change to pay the cleaner.

12. **280 km** - outskirts of GELIBOLU. The Dardanelles is visible on your left. Many first-time Australian and New Zealand tourists mistake Gelibolu for Gallipoli. It is the largest town in the region, but is some 60 kilometres away from the battlefields, so do not plan to stay here. However, it is a pretty little town and worth a rest stop. Try the fish shops near the harbour.

13. 321 km - notice the signs indicating the Mil Park turn-off to your right, adjacent to a small bay. From here you can either turn right and follow the signs into the park and to the Kabatepe Information Centre (about 7 kilometres) or proceed straight ahead to ECEABAT (about 4 kilometres). From Eceabat it is just a short ferry crossing to Çanakkale.

NOTE:

a. Petrol stations en route are plentiful, although petrol is more expensive than in Australia.

b. Be careful if you travel this route during the hours of darkness as the street lighting is poor and the lane lines are often unmarked.

c. Watch carefully for intersections as they often appear with no prior warning.

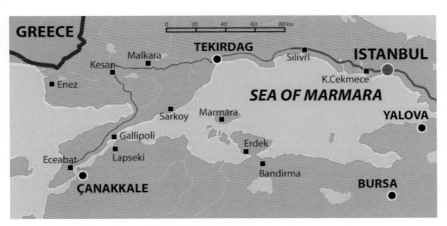

Route from Istanbul to the battlefields of Gallipoli. *(Image by Mark Wahlert)*

SECTION 16: A TOUR OF THE ANZAC BATTLEFIELD

PRIOR TO DEPARTURE

Before departing for their first tour of the battlefield, visitors should prepare a backpack containing useful and essential items such as: sunscreen, sunglasses, hat or wet weather gear (depending on season), map, guidebook, camera, wallet or purse, water and lunch. It may be sensible to wear long pants and a long-sleeved top, especially for those who intend to do some walking 'off the beaten track'.

DIY TOUR

Suggested route. The suggested 'do it yourself' (DIY) tourist route described below is designed to enable visitors to make the most of their time on the battlefields. It is structured to offer both a standard route, containing thirteen stands, and some additional (optional) walks and drives. This section of the book contains directions to each stand (as the various routes are not always obvious from the signage in the park), a fold-out map of Anzac and an explanation of what happened at each stand and what to look for.

Driving the route. For those with a car, the route commences at the Eceabat ferry terminal. From this point, visitors should follow the map (guide map or stick map) through each stand. This route is about 40 kilometres from Eceabat and back and lasts around half a day for a quick visit to the main stands and a full day if some of the optional walks are included. For those who have the time, two to three days should allow coverage of most, if not all, of the suggested locations. Drivers should take care to:

1. Reset the car's odometer to '0' as they come off the ferry at Eceabat (or, if they are staying on the western side of the Dardanelles, start the journey at Eceabat). The guide below is based on **starting the tour from Eceabat**.

2. Note that, while most of the Gallipoli park now has bitumen roads, large areas of the roadway are of very poor quality, with deep potholes, sections washed away and debris on the road. At various times, most notably around Anzac Day, the roads can be congested with convoys of large buses. Take care driving throughout the park area, especially in bad weather or after rain.

GALLIPOLI STICK MAP

36 km	**Eceabat**	
29.8 km	**Junction.** Turn left to Eceabat	
23.7 km	**Stand 13 - Chunuk Bair.** Follow signs to Eceabat	
22 km	**Stand 11 – The Nek.** Turn left down track	
21.8 km	**Stand 10 – Turkish Memorial.** Right side of road	
21.6 km	**Stand 9 - Quinn's Post.** On left side of road	
20.9 km	**Stand 8 - Johnston's Jolly**	
20.6 km	**Stand 7 – Lone Pine.** On left after bend. Watch for signs to Lone Pine Cemetery on the left	
17.8 km	**Brighton Beach.** Turn left. Follow sign to Kemalyeri	
16.1 km	**Stand 6 – Shell Green.** Turn left down track	
15.4 km	**Stand 4 - Shrapnel Valley.** Turn left down track	
15.2 km	**Stand 3 – Anzac Cove**	
14.9 km	**Stand 2 – Ari Burnu**	
14.4 km	**Stand 1 - North Beach.** Do a U-turn.	
11 km	**Brighton Beach Information Centre.** Continue on	
10.2 km	**Turn right for Kabatepe Information Centre & Museum** At cross-roads junction on the right	
3.5 km	**Turn left.** Follow signs to *Kemalyeri* & *Conkbayiri*	
0km	**Eceabat Ferry Terminal** Reset your odometer to 0. Drive north following the signs to Istanbul	

Stick Map.

Take care on the roads around the battlefield.

Walking the route. For those who would like to walk the route, the start-point is at Stand 1 - North Beach. Walking the suggested route through all thirteen stands should take the better part of a day (depending on the pace of walking and how long walkers linger at the various sites). This excludes the time visitors will then need to return to their accommodation. Two to three days is suggested for those who wish to include all the optional walks.

Alternative/optional walks/drives. A number of alternative walks and drives are suggested from the various stands that are visited. However, many of these walks are over rough, and often steep, tracks. Walkers will need good walking shoes, long trousers, a shirt with long sleeves (protection against thorns) and a large supply of water. Visitors should not attempt any of the isolated walks alone. Mobile phones do not cover the entire park and, when walkers reach their destination, they will still need to return to their car in its original location (hopefully) at the start of the walk.

Signage. The road signs around the battlefields can be quite confusing as the Allied and Turkish forces used different names to describe the same locations. Around the Gallipoli park area there are both Turkish signs and wooden ones in English erected by the CWGC, such as the one below. This guide uses both signs to aid the visitor travel the battlefield and, where appropriate, includes photographs.

CWGC road signs.

ROUTE TO AND AROUND THE BATTLEFIELD

Those staying at Çanakkale should take the ferry to Eceabat as this guide uses odometer readings from the Eceabat ferry terminal. From here, visitors should follow the stick map to the Kabatepe Information Centre and Museum, then either the stick map or the guide map on the inside back cover.

STAND 1 - NORTH BEACH (14.4 KM)

Direction to the stand. Follow the stick map from Eceabat to Stand 1, which is just over 14 kilometres from the Eceabat ferry terminal. Walk down to the Anzac Wall indicated in the picture above.

The terrain. The North Beach Commemorative Site is a fitting location for the Anzac Day dawn service each year as it was around this location that the Anzac legend was

North Beach today.

North Beach late 1915.

born at dawn on 25 April 1915. Stand near the Anzac Wall, take out your map and locate each of the features as they are described. Terrain played a vital role at Gallipoli and, in many ways, shaped the campaign. Being able to locate the key features now will aid your understanding of the campaign as we walk through each of the stands. Look out to sea. To your half left is Ari Burnu (Stand 2). It was here that the first boat touched shore around 4.30 a.m. on the first day.

Look inland and directly ahead towards the feature that dominates the landscape—the Sphinx. Having arrived from Egypt, most of the Anzacs were familiar with the real Sphinx and, in typically Australian fashion, gave this dominating natural feature its

nickname. There were, however, also practical reasons for such nicknames. There were few maps, and those that did exist were old and of limited use. Initially, troops had to rely on locally made sketches which used hastily devised nicknames to identify prominent points.

To your half left on the skyline is Walker's Ridge (Stand 12), named after Brigadier Harold Walker from the New Zealand Brigade. Walker's Ridge runs away from you to the east and ends at The Nek (Stand 11). The green hill to your half right is Plugge's Plateau (Stand 5), named after New Zealand Colonel Arthur Plugge. Plugge's Plateau runs to your right down to Ari Burnu (Stand 2). Just to the left of the green hill is a

The Sphinx from North Beach.

dominant brown cliff face which is actually the rear (or north-eastern section) of Plugge's Plateau. Moving to your left, Plugge's Plateau ends in a low, brown ridge. This is the Razor Edge and connects Plugge's Plateau with Russell's Top (Stand 12a), named after the commander of the New Zealand Mounted Rifles, Brigadier Andrew Russell, who established his headquarters there.

All of these locations, to which you can walk on this tour, are points on spurs that connect to the Sari Bair range. The first spur, known as the First Ridge, runs from the Baby 700 feature (Stand 12b) across the saddle known as The Nek (Stand 11) onto a finger-shaped plateau called Russell's Top (Stand 12a) and down to Plugge's

Plateau (Stand 5). This ridgeline, and the spurs that jut out towards the coast like probing fingers, completely dominated the area around North Beach and Anzac Cove and made the priority task of the landing troops very clear: 'capture the high ground.' The Official Historian, Charles Bean, described the topography around North Beach in daunting terms:

In front of them a small area of rough ground was shut in by bare yellow precipices rising at 300 yards from the beach. …The ridge led down to the beach in only two places - at either end of the semicircle - by the steep slopes of Plugge's [Plateau] on the right, and by a tortuous spur (Walker's Ridge) on the left. Between the two, exactly

LANDING OF THE COVERING FORCE

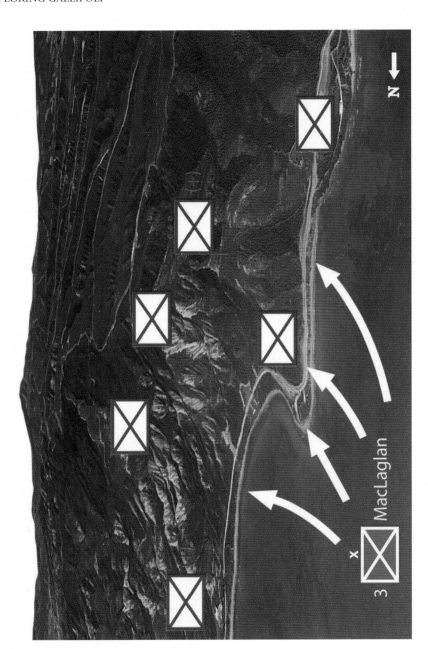

The Anzac battlefield.

in the middle of the semicircle of cliffs, there had once been a third spur, but the weather had eaten it away. Its bare gravel face stood out, for all the world like that of a Sphinx, sheer above the middle of the valley... To the Australians from that day it was the 'Sphinx'.

The Second Ridge was also important as it defined much of the Australian front line for most of the campaign. From its southern point it extended from just north of Gaba Tepe up towards Lone Pine (Stand 7), then across the 400 Plateau through key Anzac locations such as Johnston's Jolly (Stand 8), Courtney's and Steele's Posts (Stand 8b), and Quinn's Post (Stand 9). The First and Second Ridges joined near The Nek (Stand 11), then ran north-east towards the heights of Chunuk Bair (Stand 13).

What happened here? The Australians and New Zealanders who landed at Gallipoli belonged to the newly formed Australian and New Zealand Army Corps, later shortened to ANZAC, under the command of General Birdwood. Two divisions made up Birdwood's command: the 1st Australian Infantry Division (1 Aust Div) under Major General Bridges, and a combined New Zealand and Australian Division (NZ&A Div) under Major General Godley. The plan for the landing involved the 3rd Australian Brigade (part of 1st Australian Division) going ashore in two waves to act as the Covering Force. The role of the 3rd Brigade was to secure the beachhead for the arrival of the remainder of the force.

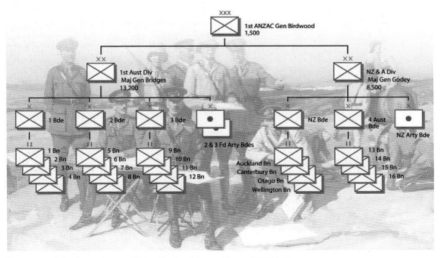

Structure of the Australian and New Zealand Army Corps (ANZAC).

The initial landing occurred just before dawn (around 4.30 a.m.) on 25 April 1915. The first wave consisted of 1,500 troops from the 3rd Australian Brigade who landed at various points on the coast from Fisherman's Hut (just north of North Beach), to the southern edge of Anzac Cove, with the majority coming ashore around Ari Burnu (which represents the southern end of North Beach). While many Australians today have romantic notions of the Anzac landing, to any observer watching the troops disembark that morning, it would have looked very confused and uncoordinated. While in the half-light of dawn it was difficult to make out details of the terrain, it was becoming increasingly obvious to the men that they had landed in the wrong place. They were, in fact, about three kilometres too far north. (For a discussion of why the Anzacs landed in the wrong place, see Section 4: The Landings.) This confusion was exacerbated by the fact that there were no maps and the area they now found themselves in was largely unknown. In addition, the boats had become mixed up and units were scattered along the shoreline. Worst of all, the enemy had the audacity to fire on them.

Those who made it ashore dashed across the open ground under fire until they found cover in the dead ground at the base of the ridgeline. Most men just kept low, unsure of what to do next. Eventually more troops arrived and their non-commissioned officers and platoon commanders rallied the men, began an arduous climb up the ridgeline to 'get to the Turks' and organised local attacks to capture enemy positions. Several groups rushed up the side of Plugge's Plateau, others scaled the impossibly steep sides of the Sphinx, while another charged a Turkish post near Fisherman's Hut.

The enemy facing the Anzac landing came from Major Ismet's *2nd Battalion, 27th Regiment*, which had its headquarters at Gaba Tepe and the task of covering a large section of the west coast of the Peninsula. Under Major Ismet's command was Captain Faik's *4th Company*, which was responsible for the area north of Gaba Tepe. Faik's company had three platoons, each of about sixty to seventy men. Faik deployed a platoon at Fisherman's Hut, another on Plugge's Plateau and the third in depth back on the Second Ridge, with a gun battery in support on the 400 Plateau, near the Lonesome Pine.

While the enemy around Ari Burnu and Plugge's Plateau were quickly overwhelmed, further north along North Beach the first of many tragedies occurred. The boats carrying 140 Australians from A Company, 7th Battalion, came under heavy enemy fire from Fisherman's Hut. Only thirty-five men made it ashore. The Turkish commander had:

ordered firing to be opened at 1300 metres. ... Some of the enemy troops were hit and stayed in the craft. Those who were not hit jumped into the sea and only five or ten men escaped by getting into our dead area.

Even the field ambulances that came ashore in the first waves were not immune to fire. The Western Australian 3rd Field Ambulance suffered seventeen casualties before it even left the beach. One soldier from the 3rd Brigade described his experience landing near North Beach:

We are now within a mile of the shore and the din has increased . . . the whole side of the mountains seems to be sending forth tongues of flame and the bullets fairly rain upon us . . . the water is churned up from rifle fire, machine-guns, Maxims, shrapnel and common shells . . . seven of the boys in our boat are killed and God knows how many in the others.

While the combined fire from the enemy positions inflicted a number of casualties on the Australians during and immediately after the landing, it was not the slaughter that many histories and personal accounts have made out. Most of the casualties on that first day were actually incurred later as the men attempted to push inland. And enemy fire was not the only threat to life during the landing. Some of the men, nervous and eager to escape the Turkish bullets now striking their boats, jumped overboard and drowned; dragged down by the 35-kilogram weight of their ammunition and equipment. A few were also hit by 'friendly fire' in the half-light of dawn. Such was the confusion on that morning.

By 8.00 a.m. all of the 3rd Brigade's 4,000 men were ashore and had cleared most of the enemy from the heights. The fight had now moved inland to the Second Ridge where resistance was stiffening and the Australian received most of their casualties. By the end of that first day, about 2,000 casualties were either evacuated or awaiting evacuation on the beaches. Many were killed and left where they lay as their mates fought a desperate battle for the Second Ridge. Others disappeared in the deep valleys and crevices and were never found.

DID THE TURKS HAVE MACHINE-GUNS TO OPPOSE THE LANDING?

By the time of the Allied attack on the Dardanelles in early 1915, stocks of the excellent German variant of the Maxim gun, the Maschinengewehr 08 (MG08), and the export version, the MG09, were slowly making their way into the Turkish infantry battalions. By mid-1915, while the Maxim had become the standard machine-gun of the Turkish forces at Gallipoli, the Turkish forces were still suffering a critical shortage of a wide variety of equipment, including machine-guns.

Controversy surrounds the question as to whether the Turkish infantry deployed near the Anzac landing sites on the morning of 25 April, had any machine guns in support. Certainly there is no shortage of personal accounts from soldiers who landed on that morning describing being fired on by 'Maxims' or 'bursts of MG fire'. Others even mention kicking 'over a Turk machine-gun' or seeing 'a dead Turk lying next to his Maxim'. Some authors and historians have even described where these machine-guns were sited, such as at Gaba Tepe, Ari Burnu, Walker's Ridge and Fisherman's Hut.

The problem is that many Turkish historians and the official Turkish records refute the Australians' claims of their landing being opposed by machine-guns. And, more recently, an excellent article in the Australian War Memorial's magazine, *Wartime* (Issue 50), casts even more doubt on the presence of Turkish machine-guns at the landing. Certainly the Turks appear to have brought up machine-guns soon after the landing to halt the Australian advance. There are numerous reports of a 'gun at Fisherman's Hut' (including an account from the Official War Historian), of troops receiving machine-gun fire from what became known as Battleship Hill, of Australian's being halted in their southern movement by 'machine-gun fire from Gabe Tepe', of the 3rd Field Ambulance 'receiving MG fire onto North Beach', and the Turks being supported by 'machine-gun fire in their attack mid-morning'. The bottom-line is simply that we do not know for sure whether the Turks had machine-guns to oppose the landing at Anzac.

Top image: The Maschinengewehr 08 (MG08)
(Image by Mark Wahlert)

With the First Ridge secured, and the second being secured, men and stores could be landed at Anzac Cove with only minimal interference from the enemy. North Beach remained dangerous until after the August offensive when it became a relatively safe rear area and was developed into a major supply base and hospital. While it remained within range of Turkish snipers and artillery, and casualties were commonplace, men regularly came down from the forward trenches for a swim and some relief from the tedium and tension of the front line. For example, Private Richard Bulkeley of the 3rd Battalion, recalled:

> I hadn't had a change of underclothes for nearly two months, so when Sid found some (in one of the dead's back packs) we decided to go down to the

beach for a swim and change. The beach is a far more dangerous place than the firing line, except when we are actually under attack. Every day there are a good few casualties and it's not uncommon for a hundred to be hit in one day. It's mainly down to 'Beachy Bill' (a Turk gun down at Gabe Tepe). Up until the end of July this gun was alone responsible for just over 900 casualties.

Things to see. North Beach is a good location from which to get your bearings before starting on your tour. Read the panels along the wall near the road and then relate your map to the key features described above. This orientation to the ground will aid your understanding of what happened at the stands that follow.

North Beach from Plugge's Plateau. *(AWM A01867)*

STAND 2 - ARI BURNU (14.9 KM)

Direction to the stand. Walk/drive back the way you came for about 400 metres until you arrive at Ari Burnu Cemetery (it is at the end of North Beach and is the headland you see from the North Beach wall as you look south along the beach). This is where it all started. Walk into the pretty little cemetery that marks the point where the first boat-load of Australians stepped ashore early on the morning of 25 April 1915. After you have had a quick look around, move to the top of the steps leading down to the beach from the retaining wall and look inland.

The terrain. This cemetery, the centre of the landings on 25 April, is dominated by the high ground immediately to your front (Plugge's Plateau – Stand 5). The ridgeline that runs from Plugge's Plateau away to your right is MacLagan's Ridge, and the knoll on that ridge, just to the right of the cemetery's monument, is Ari Burnu knoll. Both of these features were occupied by the enemy on the morning of 25 April, affording them excellent observation and fields of fire down on to the beach. To your half left is the Sphinx; the ridge on the skyline to the left of the Sphinx is Walker's Ridge (Stand 12). Moving to your right from the Sphinx, follow the ridgeline until you see where it dips

ARI BURNU POINT

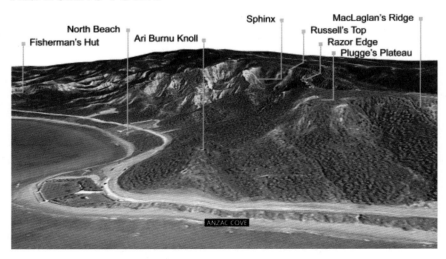

Ari Burnu Point. *(Image by Mark Wahlert)*

behind Plugge's Plateau. This is the Razor Edge which connects Plugge's Plateau with Russell's Top (Stand 12a).

Walk down the steps to the beach, then left to the edge of the cemetery. That stretch of beach to your front is Anzac Cove. The point at the southern end of Anzac Cove (where there are two collapsed World War II bunkers) is Hell Spit (or Queensland Point). Behind and to the right of Hell Spit is Gaba Tepe. The beach connecting Gaba Tepe with Hell Spit is Brighton Beach, the original planned landing site for the Anzacs.

What happened here? Many of the boats from the Covering Force landed at dawn on 25 April in the area where you are now standing. Defending this area was Second Lieutenant Muharrem's platoon. The platoon had nine sections of infantry, each of about seven to ten men. Muharrem's headquarters and most of his platoon were dug in on Plugge's Plateau (the hill immediately to your east that dominates this position). In addition, he had deployed section-sized observation posts on Hell Spit (the southern end of Anzac Cove) and Ari Burnu knoll (the knoll between the top of Plugge's Plateau and Ari Burnu). Ari Burnu knoll has been undermined by road works in recent years and was far more prominent in 1915. There was also a third section in depth on the First Ridge at Russell's Top (Stand 12a). Whether Muharrem also had machine-guns is unknown (see Sidebar).

Just before 4.30 a.m., as dawn began to break and the initial Australian landing parties were about 25 yards from the shore, Muharrem's platoon opened fire. One wag from the 11th Battalion was heard to comment, 'They better cut that out or someone might get killed!' Captain Leane of the 11th Battalion later wrote:

> The boat I was in landed on the point. There were three boats to the left of us containing 9th Battalion men, most of whom were killed or wounded in the boat on the extreme left.

As the men came ashore around Ari Burnu there was confusion. They had landed in the wrong place, were all mixed up and many of the officers were separated from their men. Most of the men were taking shelter from enemy fire behind a high bank. Eventually one of the officers, LT Talbot Smith, in charge of the 10th Battalion Scouts, was heard to yell 'Come on boys! They can't hit you.' He was the first to lead his men in a wild charge up Plugge's yelling 'Come on Australians, give them the bayonet.' One member of this charge, Sergeant Cheney wrote home 'I was lost in the wild mob, in the wildest of charges. Everybody had taken leave of their senses. Although I know what fear is, it left me as we went straight up that rugged, rocky, precipice.'

While the Turks maintained a steady stream of fire from their positions all around where you now stand, they were too few in number to stem the tide of the Australian troops now coming ashore. That little beach in front of you was crammed with the boats and men of the 9th, 10th and 11th battalions. They were nervous, excited and keen to get at the enemy.

While we will never really know who the first to land was, Charles Bean, stated that it was probably the 9th Battalion's Lieutenant Duncan Chapman.

Things to see. Ari Burnu was used as a cemetery from the day of the landing as it was under constant enemy observation and fire and, therefore, could be used for little else. There are 254 servicemen buried or commemorated in this cemetery. Among those are 82 men from the Light Horse, most from the 8th and 10th Light Horse Regiments who were killed at the ill-fated charge at The Nek on 6 August (refer to Stand 11). Two of those are Lance Corporal Lindsay Chipper, 28, and his brother Trooper Ross Chipper, 31, both from the 10th Light Horse Regiment (plots E15 and E19). A number of 9th Light Horse Regiment men who were killed during the August offensive are also buried in this cemetery. Among them is their Commanding Officer, Lieutenant Colonel Albert Miell (plot A17), who was killed while directing fire from his regiment's trench-line on Russell's Top in support of the charge at The Nek, and Trooper Seager (plot A18), one of the youngest members of the Light Horse, who was killed on 7 August aged 17.

As you exit the Ari Burnu Cemetery, walk south along the side of the road a few metres until you see a monument on your right. On this monument is a tribute from Mustafa Kemal Atatürk to his former enemies. Atatürk commanded the Turkish regiment that faced the Anzacs at Gallipoli and was President of Turkey at the time these words were attributed to him in 1934.

The view from the Turkish outpost on Plugge's Plateau as the first boats of the 3rd Brigade landed at Ari Burnu on 25 April 1915.

STAND 3 - ANZAC COVE (ANZAK KOYU) AND BEACH CEMETERY (15.2 KM)

Direction to the stand. From Ari Burnu you can either walk along Anzac Cove itself or along the road to Stand 3, about 500 metres to the south. You will know when you have arrived as this is one of the better signed locations on the Peninsula. Move to a position just in from the Anzac Cove sign where you can look north, back up the beach towards Ari Burnu.

Anzac Cove looking towards Ari Burnu.
(AWM P01130.001)

The terrain. As you look north, identify Ari Burnu knoll and Plugge's Plateau (Stand 5). The ridge to your right that runs up to Plugge's Plateau is MacLagan's Ridge, named after the commander of the 3rd Brigade, Lieutenant Colonel Ewen Sinclair-MacLagan. In 1915, the area between the beach and MacLagan's Ridge resembled a mining camp rather than the rear area of an army corps.

Dugouts and lean-to shelters were scattered over the entire area. Anzac Headquarters was located about halfway along the Cove and just in from the beach. Numerous other supporting or administrative units were also sited close to the Cove. There was even a bomb factory that made hand grenades out of jam tins, nails and explosives.

While this entire area was subjected to constant enemy shelling which inflicted many casualties, it was one of the few locations early in the campaign that was not under enemy observation. To the north, enemy forces on the various hills had a clear view of North Beach while, to the south, Brighton Beach was easily observed from Gaba Tepe.

Note that the road has changed the landscape of the Cove compared to the way it would have looked in 1915, and that the spoil from the road has reduced the size of the beach in places, making it difficult to imagine how cluttered and crammed this entire area was. One correspondent at the time likened the scene at Anzac Cove to '... a gigantic shipwreck. It looked as if the whole force and all the guns and material had not been landed, but had been washed ashore.'

What happened here? Anzac Cove is synonymous with the Anzac campaign. It is certainly the best known location on Gallipoli. It was here that the greater proportion of the main body landed on 25 April, where most of the supplies and reinforcements came ashore, and where the wounded and sick were evacuated. Its central location and degree of protection from snipers made Anzac Cove the heart of Anzac through which was pumped its lifeblood of supplies and men. Originally this small cove had no name. However, a few days after the landing, Lieutenant General Birdwood, the commander of the Anzac Corps, gave it the name it still bears today.

Soon after the landing, several piers were built to handle the constant flow of supplies in and wounded out. The longest and most famous of these was Watson's Pier, named after Lieutenant Stanley Watson, the second-in-command of the Australian Divisional Engineers, who supervised its construction. The Cove was a popular spot for the troops to swim, although it was routinely shelled by the Turks. One soldier wrote in a letter home that 'we have not had our clothes off for five weeks and it was most pleasant to strip off and have a dip in the sea. The weather here is glorious just at present and I am in the best of health.'

Dugouts at Anzac Cove. *(AWM CO1129)*

Things to see. About halfway along the Cove, opposite a large drain and wash-away, is where Watson's Pier once stood. This pier was the longest, busiest and most famous of the piers constructed at Anzac. Immediately above the pier was General Birdwood's headquarters (unrecognisable now due to the construction of the road).

Looking north along Anzac Cove.

From the Anzac Cove stone (see picture), walk about 25 metres north until you come to a path on your left. Follow the path around to the south.

Be careful of loose edges caused by erosion as it is sheer drop down to the beach. After about 150 metres you will enter Beach Cemetery. This area was used as a cemetery from the first day as it was under constant fire from Gaba Tepe. The casualty clearing station was also located nearby, meaning that many of the graves are of those who were wounded throughout Anzac only to die after they had been evacuated to the beach.

Beach Cemetery holds the remains of 391 Commonwealth servicemen, including 295 Australians and 22 New Zealanders. The most famous person interred here is Private John Simpson Kirkpatrick, 'the man with the donkey'. As you walk down the few steps in front of the memorial stone, turn right and walk north (back towards Ari Burnu) a few paces. One of the first headstones you will come across is simply marked '*John Simpson Kirkpatrick. Served as 202 Private J. Simpson, Aust Army Medical Corps*'. Simpson was aged just 22 when he was killed by enemy fire on 19 May 1915 as he was bringing down a wounded man with his donkey. He was just one of many medics and stretcher-bearers who assisted the wounded, although he is undoubtedly the best known.

Simpson's grave at Beach Cemetery.

Also buried here is Captain Edward (Bob) Bage (plot I.D.7), second-in-command of the 3rd Field Company, Australian Divisional Engineers. Bage, aged 27, was famous in Australia as a member of Mawson's 1911–13 Antarctic Expedition, during which he led a team on a perilous 1,000-kilometre journey towards the Pole. He was killed near Lone Pine on 2 May while marking out a trench. The machine-gun fire in the area was so heavy that his body could not be recovered until nightfall.

STAND 4 - SHRAPNEL VALLEY CEMETERY (15.4 KM)

Direction to the stand. Almost opposite the Anzac Cove sign is the entrance to Shrapnel Valley Cemetery. The actual cemetery is about 150 metres along the track. Follow the track and, on arrival at the cemetery, walk to the tree in the centre of the cemetery.

Shrapnel Valley Cemetery.

The terrain. Shrapnel Valley Cemetery is situated at the beginning of Shrapnel Valley or, as some refer to it, Shrapnel Gully. The Gully follows the path of a small creek bed up to the base of Braund's Hill, which was named after the commander of the 2nd Battalion, Lieutenant Colonel George Braund, who was shot and killed by his own sentry on 4 May. The path then splits into Monash Valley, which travels north-east behind Second Ridge, and Bridges' Road which continues east along the southern side of Braund's Hill and connects to the Second Ridge near Steele's Post (see Optional Walks 5a and 5b and map). These paths were the Anzacs' highway and all along the sides of the gullies and valleys were camps, depots, dugouts and gun positions. The entire area is dominated by the heights of Plugge's Plateau (Stand 5) and MacLagan's Ridge.

What happened here? Shrapnel Valley was the scene of much fighting

on the morning of the landings as men of the Australian Covering Force clashed with the Turkish infantry guarding this section of the beach. Both Shrapnel Valley and the gully it leads into, Monash Valley, became the main supply routes for the Anzacs. Along this track, which for most of the campaign was subjected to constant shelling, poured the men and supplies landed at Anzac Cove and destined for the Anzac front line.

Not only was the entire length of this valley under constant bombardment, but from the day of the landing it was also exposed to Turkish snipers. After numerous men had been killed by sniper fire, sandbag walls were erected along the worst sections. Men would then dash from cover to cover. Eventually a deep communications trench was dug which offered better protection. Regardless of this, the Turks still managed to pick off the occasional unwary or careless digger. The Turks retained this advantage as the Anzacs were never able to capture all the high ground and, from such places as Dead Man's Ridge and the Bloody Angle, Turkish snipers could fire at the constant stream of reinforcements and men carrying all form of supplies to the front along the valleys.

Private Ion (Jack) Idriess, later to become one of Australia's most prolific authors, wrote on 22 May 1915:

A party of us volunteered for a sapping job last night. We left camp at eleven and followed the road, which is the gully bottom, meandering up to the firing line. Across the gully are built sandbag barricades which shield a man just a little from the death-traps along the road. We would bend our backs and run to a big barricade, lean against the bags until we panted back our breath, then dive around the corner and rush for the next barricade… [The Turks have] expert snipers, unerring shots who have killed God only knows how many of our men when coming along the road.

Things to see. Major Hugh Quinn, 15th Battalion, is buried here in Plot III.C.21 (about ten paces from the cemetery entrance to your half right). Quinn, an amateur heavyweight boxer and an accountant from Queensland, had commanded Charlie Company from its formation in Australia. On 29 April, he and his company moved to reinforce a section of the front that was under constant pressure from the Turks. Quinn was shot in the head and killed on 29 May while repelling an attack, the first company commander in the battalion to be killed in action. He was 27 years old. The area where he was killed became known as Quinn's Post.

Shrapnel Valley Cemetery contains the bodies of almost 700 men. It was used as a cemetery during the campaign and after the war other graves in the vicinity were added.

STAND 5 - PLUGGE'S PLATEAU

Direction to the stand. As you look at the Shrapnel Valley Cemetery monument, move to the left of the cemetery where you will find an access path that leads up the hill behind the cemetery to Plugge's Plateau. While it is only about 600 metres to the top, it is a rough path and steep in sections. Do not attempt this unless you are in at least reasonable physical condition. It will take you about 15 minutes to reach the top. Walk to a position just past the cemetery where you can overlook Ari Burnu, Anzac Cove and North Beach.

Path to Plugge's Plateau.

The terrain. As is clear from this position, Plugge's Plateau dominates both Anzac Cove and the North Beach area, affording the Turks excellent observation and fields of fire. On a clear day you can see as far north as Suvla Bay, the location of the landing of the British IX Corps during the August offensive, and to Gaba Tepe in the south.

Follow the track to the left of the cemetery to the opposite end of Plugge's Plateau (eastern side). Be careful, as it will end with a sharp drop into Rest Gully, which was used by Anzac troops as a rest area due to the protection afforded by the high sides of the surrounding hills. Find a good spot to take in the vista to the east and locate the Sphinx to your half left (north-north-east). Just to the right of the Sphinx, on the ridge behind it, you will notice a brown scar with a sign and wooden rails: this is Walker's Ridge (Stand 12). The cream-coloured monument on the skyline to the right is the Turkish *57th Regiment* Memorial (Stand 10). The green, scrub-covered area in between these two points is Russell's Top (Stand 12A), which is connected to Plugge's Plateau by the Razor Edge (see image below). Do not attempt to cross onto Russell's Top via the Razor Edge. To your right you should be able to see where Shrapnel Valley runs up to Braund's Hill and then splits into Bridges' Road and Monash Valley. To the right of Braund's Hill, on the Second Ridge, you might just be able to see the white top of the Lone Pine Memorial.

VIEW FROM PLUGGE'S PLATEAU

View from rear of Plugge's Plateau.

What happened here? Plugge's Plateau is named after Colonel Arthur Plugge, Commanding Officer of the Auckland Battalion, whose headquarters was briefly sited on this hill. It was also used as an artillery position as there were few flat areas suitable for artillery deployment in the Anzac area. As described in the narrative for Stand 2 - Ari Burnu, on the morning of the landing, this area was occupied by several sections of Turkish infantry from Second Lieutenant Muharrem's platoon. Looking down on Ari Burnu and North Beach, you can see the perfect fields of fire enjoyed by these troops in the breaking dawn. The Turkish position was well established, consisting of a main trench along the top of Plugge's Plateau facing the beaches below, several smaller trenches supporting this main trench, and a communications trench which connected them all. A small camp had been established in Shrapnel Valley below, a rest point for off-duty troops. Evidence of the Turkish trenches is still visible today.

Once his section was forced to retire from its entrenched position near Ari Burnu, Muharrem's men continued to fire from their positions here on Plugge's Plateau. Some years later, Turkish cartridge cases were still being unearthed in this vicinity. Below, at Ari Burnu, an Australian lieutenant from the 10th Battalion yelled, 'Come on, boys! They

can't hit you!' and a 'mad rush of a mixed batch of 9th, 10th, and 11th Battalion lads started up the steep slope of Plugge's Plateau to seize the heights.'

A Scene from George Lambert's painting, *The Landing*. This painting shows the West Australians from the 11th Battalion climbing up to Plugge's Plateau from North Beach. *(AWM ART02873)*

Muharrem's troops kept firing on the advancing Australians until, low on ammunition and on the point of being overrun, he ordered a withdrawal. Just as the Turks started to move back, the first of the Australians reached the top of Plugge's Plateau and a short but bloody close-quarter fight ensued with rifle and bayonet. One Australian later wrote home that, as he reached the top of the hill he:

saw three Turks firing down onto the beach. There was nobody between them and me . . . so I dropped to one knee and let him have it. I couldn't well miss. I saw him drop and when I got up to him I found that I had hit him fair between the eyes.

Plugge's Plateau was the first major feature to fall to the Australians. Sadly, this was not the only 'first'. Captain Annear from the 11th Battalion was shot in the head, becoming the first Australian officer to die at Gallipoli. Despite the Official Historian's attempts to play down the shooting of prisoners, this certainly occurred at Gallipoli. In fact, it was just after the capture of Plugge's Plateau that one of the first incidents of the shooting of prisoners by Australians occurred. One small group of men from the 10th Battalion chased a group of Turks down the side of Plugge's Plateau and into Shrapnel Valley. Surrendering as the Australians were about to catch them, the Turks were quickly shot and the Australians hurried on. Such incidents occurred on both sides. The Turks were also in no mood to take prisoners and a number of Australians and New Zealanders were similarly dispatched when captured that day.

Later on the first day, members of the Otago Battalion were rushed onto Plugge's Plateau to defend it against a possible Turkish breakthrough. Across the line the Anzacs were under severe pressure from an intense Turkish counter-attack. Both Pine Ridge and Baby 700 had fallen with high Anzac casualties, and the whole perimeter was under threat. The Otago Battalion dug in under constant fire from enemy artillery and snipers. This position had to be held at all costs against a threatened Turkish breakthrough.

Soon after the landing, a sap was constructed up to Plugge's Plateau from Ari Burnu. A 'sap' was a dug-in road or path that offered those using it protection from snipers and shrapnel. The sap to Plugge's Plateau allowed men, materiel and artillery to climb the side of the hill in relative safety. Eventually this sap was extended from Anzac Cove to the outposts on the northern edge of North Beach. In places, these saps were three metres wide and three metres deep, allowing mules to pass one another without leaving the sap.

Things to see. Kneel or lie down to see the excellent firing position this spot afforded the Turks as the Australians came ashore on 25 April. From here accurate rifle fire could hit targets about halfway down Anzac Cove and the southern end of North Beach. In addition, if a Maxim machine-gun was located here, it could cover all of Anzac Cove and interlock with any fire coming from Turkish positions on Fisherman's Hut (to the northern end of North Beach). Anzac Headquarters was just below where you are standing (between Plugge's Plateau and Ari Burnu), although any evidence of its location has been destroyed by roadworks.

Plugge's Plateau Cemetery is the smallest at Gallipoli with only 21 men buried here. Half these were killed on the first day of the campaign. Three others were artillerymen killed by Turkish counter-battery fire.

OPTIONAL WALK 5A – SHRAPNEL VALLEY – BRIDGES' ROAD

Duration: 1 hr one-way.
Distance: 1.2 km. **Difficulty**: Hard.
Rough track, overgrown gully, steep ascent at the end.

From Shrapnel Valley Cemetery, walk east along the valley. The first offshoot to the left is Rest Gully, but keep moving straight ahead. After a walk of around 20 minutes you will come to the base of Braund's Hill and the junction with Monash Valley (to your left and north) and Bridges' Road (to your right and east). The walk up Bridges' Road is another 40 minutes or so and takes you past the 4th Battalion Parade Ground Cemetery (high on your left) and the 400 Plateau feature on your right. There is a steep climb at the end up towards the front line, which emerges near Courtney's and Steele's Posts. Ensure that you wear long pants, a long-sleeved shirt and sturdy shoes as much of this path is overgrown with thorn bushes.

OPTIONAL WALK 5B – SHRAPNEL VALLEY – MONASH VALLEY

Duration: 2 hrs one-way.
Distance: 1.5 km. **Difficulty:** Hard.
Rough track, overgrown gully, steep ascent up to the main road.

Walk east along Shrapnel Valley from the Shrapnel Valley Cemetery. After about one kilometre, the gully curves sharply to the right and, after a while, to the left. This is the spot where Shrapnel Valley changes name and becomes Monash Valley. Keep to the left and walk straight on through the valley. When, a little while later, you see the spire of the cream-coloured Turkish monument on the right-hand side high above, try to move underneath that spot. At this point you will find an indentation in the side of Monash Valley which was once the site of Quinn's Post. From here you have two options: 1) climb the steep flank of the indentation, which was the 1915 method to reach Quinn's Post; or 2) continue until the ground starts rising. You might find the gentler slope of Pope's Hill easier to climb, depending on vegetation. From the top of the ridge, regardless of where you ascended, you will eventually come across the main road. As for all walks off the main paths, ensure that you wear long pants, a long-sleeved shirt and sturdy shoes.

SHRAPNEL VALLEY, MONASH VALLEY & BRIDGES' ROAD

1 ■ Shrapnel Valley Cemetery

2 ■ Plugge's Plateau

3 ■ Braund's Hill

4 ■ 4th Bn Parade Ground Cemetery

5 ■ Lone Pine Memorial

6 ■ Quinn's Post Cemetery

7 ■ Courtney's & Steele's Post Cemetery

8 ■ Pope's Post

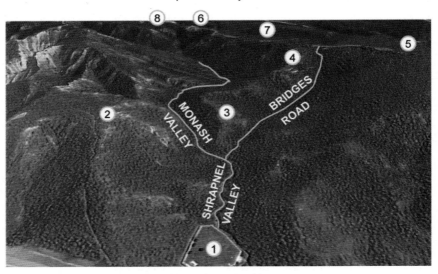

To Quinn's Post through Monash Valley. *(image by Mark Wahlert)*

STAND 6 - SHELL GREEN CEMETERY (16.1 KM)

Direction to the stand. Walk back down to Shrapnel Valley and follow the track back to the main road. About 700 metres south along the road is another track signed to Shell Green. The track from the road to Shell Green Cemetery, unlike many others, is well signposted. Follow the track about 500 metres (you can drive if it is dry, but check the condition of the road as it is often washed out in sections).

Shell Green Cemetery

The terrain. The area where you now stand, Shell Green, earned its name on 26 April as the place where the Anzacs were subjected to an intense artillery bombardment. The area offers excellent views to both the north and the south. The ridgeline to the south and south-east is Bolton's Ridge, named after Lieutenant Colonel William Bolton, Commanding Officer of the 8th Battalion. This ridge represented the right flank of Anzac and its southern-most point, although observation posts such as Chatham's Post were established a few hundred metres further south to provide early warning of a surprise attack. The hilly terrain and numerous gullies at Anzac meant that there were very few suitable positions to locate Allied artillery. This was one of the few good positions. To support the guns deployed here, and the troops entrenched around Bolton's Ridge (for a large slice of the campaign this sector was defended by the 3rd Brigade), a road was laid from the beach to Shell Green. Known as Artillery Road, it was later extended up to Lone Pine to support the August offensive. Offering excellent fields of observation and fire, Shell Green was central to protecting Anzac from an attack from the south.

What happened here? Shell Green was captured by the 8th Battalion on 25 April, and used for most of the campaign as an artillery position. Artillery, or more appropriately the absence of it, was a major issue for the Anzacs at Gallipoli. As soon as it was

sufficiently light to direct artillery, the Turks commenced their bombardment of the attacking Australians around Ari Burnu. While the enemy battery around the 400 Plateau soon withdrew as it became threatened by the advancing Australians, the Turks always appeared to have the advantage when it came to artillery support. Throughout the campaign the lack of Allied artillery, and the prolific use of guns by the Turks, had an enormously demoralising effect on the Allied troops. The Allies were desperately short of nearly all forms of artillery, trench mortars, grenades and high explosive shells. On average, the Allied forces on Gallipoli were supported by about a third of the artillery available to a similar-sized force on the Western Front. The frustration born of this lack of artillery was evident in the correspondence from the front. Colonel Hobbs, then the Commander Royal Artillery for the 1st Australian Division, wrote:

We are dominated by the enemy guns and observation stations . . . and are subject to heavy shell fire at once. Our guns are badly knocked about and many casualties. It is impossible for us to discover enemy batteries which are hidden in Nullahs and behind ridges which our guns. . . cannot reach.

As a result of their lack of artillery, the Allies were overly reliant on naval gunfire support. Naval gunfire did score some initial successes. For example, on 27 April, the 15-inch guns of the *Queen Elizabeth* halted a Turkish counter-attack and, on the same day, sank a Turkish transport ship at a range of over 20 kilometres. However, the Turks soon learnt to keep out of sight of the old battleships which had poor fire control and few high explosive shells. There was also no reliable system for calling in ship-to-shore barrages, so that, unless the ships could see what was occurring on the battlefield, they were forced to fire blind—making them equally dangerous to the Anzacs.

By noon on the first day, about four Turkish artillery batteries were in action against the Anzacs and were inflicting severe casualties. One battery was located on Chunuk Bair (Stand 13) and constantly bombarded the Anzac positions on Baby 700 and The Nek. Another, firing from Scrubby Knoll on Third Ridge, fixed on the 400 Plateau and any opportunity targets in the vicinity. A third shelled anything that moved on the southern section of the Australian line, while the fourth battery at Gaba Tepe focused on the congested beach and any boats moving ashore.

To counter these Turkish guns, one Indian mountain battery came ashore in the afternoon and established itself on the 400 Plateau. While the gunners scored some stunning successes, it could not counter all four Turkish batteries and, after suffering horrendous casualties, was forced to retire. Moving and supplying the guns with ammunition in this hilly terrain was a particular problem at Anzac. To ease this burden, a road (Artillery Road) was constructed from Anzac Cove to Shell Green, and later extended up to Lone Pine to support the August offensive. Notwithstanding these Herculean efforts, the Anzac terrain considerably limited the number of positions that the gunners could use. Considering that the Turks knew all these locations, and that there were always more Turkish guns than the Anzacs could muster, the job of a 'gunner' was one of the most dangerous at Gallipoli.

The guns in action. A 9th Battery 18-pound field gun in action during a Turkish attack. *(AWM A00830)*

NAVAL GUNFIRE SUPPORT AT GALLIPOLI

The role of the navy is critical to the success of any amphibious operation. Gallipoli was no exception. The Royal Navy's role at Anzac was to land and supply the force, and to provide vital naval gunfire support. Land-based field artillery was in short supply as the Allied forces at Gallipoli were supported by about a third of the artillery available to a similar-sized force on the Western Front. Consequently, in the planning for the landings at Gallipoli, the big guns of the Royal Navy were factored in as the force's main source of fire support. However, naval gunfire support proved generally ineffective.

The terrain around Anzac suited howitzers (guns that could fire at a high elevation). Howitzers were designed so that they could hit reverse slope positions, hilltops and deep gullies – all characteristics of the Anzac battlefield. The navy's guns, while packing quite a punch, fired on a flat trajectory and could not access many of the Turkish positions, especially after the Turks learned how to position their trench-lines to minimise interference from naval gunfire. Firing off an unstable platform with poor communications to direct the fire, the naval guns could only hit some of the targets they could see from the ship and proved generally inaccurate. This did not bode well for the type of combat that was to feature at Anzac.

In numerous places the distance between the two sides was only a few metres. Large high explosive charges which fell indiscriminately around the Anzac positions, and which could not be accurately adjusted, did not bolster the confidence of the hapless Aussies and Kiwis on the ground.

There were a few examples of successful naval artillery support. For example, on 27 April, during the first Turkish counter-attack at Anzac, the enemy attacked down the seaward slope of Battleship Hill within view of the *Queen Elizabeth* which fired a salvo of six 15-in shells, halting the attack completely. The following day, the *Queen Elizabeth* sighted a company of Turks and fired a single 15-in shrapnel shell containing 24,000 pellets at relatively short range. The entire enemy party was destroyed. Also in April, a kite-balloon ship spotted a Turkish transport moving near the Narrows. The *Queen Elizabeth* fired across the peninsula at a range of about 20 km and sank the transport with her third shot.

Eventually, after three British battleships were torpedoed in May, most of the capital ships were withdrawn to safer waters, leaving the Anzacs to rely on the small number of artillery batteries supporting the force.

HMS Queen Elizabeth was one of the most modern and well-armed ships at Gallipoli (AWM G00447)

The Turks never seemed to suffer from a shortage of ammunition, despite the occasional Turkish shell exploding and sending out shards of pottery rather than steel, indicating that they had some munitions production problems. The supply of artillery shells to the Allied fronts, however, was a key concern throughout the campaign. By June the situation was so critical that ammunition was rationed to about eight rounds per gun per day.

It is interesting to note that Shell Green held the first, and possibly only, cricket game at Gallipoli in 1915. The game was part of the elaborate deception plan devised by Brigadier Brudenell White to portray 'normality' to the Turks and cover the preparations for the evacuation.

Things to see. The Shell Green Cemetery was used by the 9th and 11th Battalions and the Light Horse for most of the campaign. It contains the graves of 409 men, eleven of them unidentified. Buried here is the 11th Battalion's Private Roy Facey, aged 23 (Plot II.G.13). One of Roy's brothers, Lance Corporal Joseph Facey, 32, from the 10th Light Horse Regiment, is buried at the Embarkation Pier Cemetery. Roy and another brother, Albert, were in the same attack on Bolton's Ridge on 28 June when Roy was killed. Albert Facey was the author of *A Fortunate Life*, published in the

1980s, which covered a portion of the brothers' service at Gallipoli. The book is a gritty and honest portrayal of Facey's life in Australia and at the front and is well worth reading.

Walk behind and to the left of Shell Green Cemetery's stone monument and climb the knoll that forms part of Bolton's Ridge. From here you will have an excellent view south along Brighton Beach to Gaba Tepe, north towards Suvla Bay and north-east towards Lone Pine. Where you are standing now was the rear area of the 9th Battalion for much of the campaign and the north-west edge of Bolton's Ridge. The north side of this ridge was honeycombed with dugouts, storage tunnels and access trenches. One wag from the Australian field artillery whose dugout was sited near this spot, wrote:

I was looking out front [of] the entrance of my dug-out, thinking how peaceful everything was, when Johnny Turk opened on our trenches. Shells were bursting, and fragments scattered all about Shell Green. Just at this time some new reinforcements were eagerly collecting spent fuses and shells as mementoes. While this fusillade was on, men were walking about the Green just as usual, when one was hit by a falling fuse. Out rushed one of the reinforcement chaps, and when he saw that the man was not hurt be asked: "Want the fuse, mate?" The other looked at him calmly. "What do you think I stopped it for?" he asked.

Anzac guns and dugouts at Shell Green, showing north side of Bolton's Ridge. *(AWM P00117.005)*

About 400 metres south of where you are standing was Chatham's Post, the southern limit of the Anzac line. Named after Lieutenant Chatham of the 5th Australian Light Horse, the Post is difficult to locate due to the extent of the undergrowth. However, if you are prepared to fight the thorn bushes, drive or walk towards the Shell Green turn-off from the Brighton Beach Information Centre (the one close to the beach and the intersection of the coast and Lone Pine roads). After about one kilometre you will come to a marker delineating the southern boundary of the battlefield. Walk directly east into the bush and after about 200 metres look for a high point on the ridge to your front (Harris Ridge). While there is little to distinguish

Chatham's Post from any other aspect of the ridgeline, anyone with basic military training will identify a couple of locations on the ridge that dominate any approach from the south. You will know if you are at the right position as there remains ample evidence of Australian trenches. On one visit to this area there were still numerous .303 cartridge cases still lying just below the surface, clear depressions made by old trenches and the sun-bleached bones of a body nearby.

Looking south from Bolton's Ridge, Chatham's Post is the small knoll on the ridgeline in the top left-hand corner of the photo.

Allied .303 rifle rounds located at Chatham's Post.

Chatham's Post was made famous during the campaign by the exploits of Trooper Billy Sing of the 5th Light Horse Regiment. Billy, nicknamed 'The Assassin', was the most famous Anzac sniper at Gallipoli, with an official tally of 201. During his time at Chatham's Post he had 150 confirmed kills. The Turks considered Billy Sing such a threat that they arranged for their own champion sniper, 'Abdul the Terrible', to hunt him down. However, Abdul proved no match and Billy killed him in a sniping duel.

An observer checks the target with his periscope while two snipers wait beside him in the trench. *(AWM P01531.015)*

SNIPING AT GALLIPOLI

At Gallipoli, the Turkish, British, French and Anzac soldiers used sniping extensively. The terrain and the close proximity of the 'rear area' provided a target-rich environment for the sniper, especially the Turk. From the day of the landing the Australians were troubled by Turks sniping on them from the various hills and ridges that surrounded their positions. All ranks were vulnerable, as evidenced in the death of the Australian Commander, General Bridges, who was shot by a Turkish sniper on 15 May 1915. The Anzacs quickly employed their own snipers, utilising the Australian bushman's skills in shooting, hunting, tracking and estimating distance, all highly desirable qualities in a sniper. It was not long before the Australian snipers began to inflict as many casualties on the Turks as they had on the Anzac troops in the months following the landing.

The typical Australian sniping team consisted of two soldiers—a sniper and his spotter. While some Australians managed to bring their own rifles to Gallipoli, others obtained rare British telescopic or optical sights. Most, however, simply used the standard .303 rifle over open sights. The spotter would often employ a variety of periscope devices. The sniper team would usually leave the trenches after last light and move into its hide, or 'possie', just before dawn, remaining there all day and only returning to the lines after dark.

The most famous Australian sniper during the Gallipoli campaign was Trooper Billy Sing of the 5th Light Horse Regiment. Nicknamed 'The Assassin' or 'The Murderer' by his Regiment, Sing was a kangaroo shooter from central Queensland and a crack shot. Arriving at Anzac Cove with the rest of his unit in May 1915, he quickly earned a reputation as the deadliest shot on the Peninsula. In October, the Australian Commander, General Birdwood, officially acknowledged Private Sing's tally of 201 Turks. Soon after, General Birdwood accompanied Sing on a 'hunting' expedition and witnessed him drop a Turk at over 200 yards. Birdwood quickly complimented Sing on his accuracy, but the laconic sniper simply replied, 'I won't be claiming that one. I was aiming at another.'

General Birdwood presents award to Private Billy Sing. (AWM P01778.004)

Billy Sing was mentioned in despatches and was awarded a Distinguished Conduct Medal for conspicuous gallantry as a sniper at Anzac. He survived the remainder of the war, dying almost penniless in Brisbane in 1943, aged 57.

OPTIONAL WALK 6A – INLAND WALK TO LONE PINE

Duration: 15 mins one-way.
Distance: 1 km. **Difficulty:** Easy-medium. Well defined track, gradual ascent to Lone Pine.

An alternative walk from Shell Green runs along the old Artillery Road. While the road existed as a supply track from early in the campaign, it was improved before the August offensive to allow guns and ammunition to be hauled forward in support of the attack on Lone Pine. For part of its distance, the road follows Bolton's Ridge and skirts the southern edge of the Anzac position. It provides some magnificent views and exits just north of the Lone Pine Cemetery. Where road bends right near top of ridge was known as Brown's Dip. This was the Assembly Area for the infantry due to attack Lone Pine on 6 August, and also contained an artillery battery and a Casualty Clearance Station. Remember that, unless you have a vehicle parked near Lone Pine, you will have to walk back down again.

STAND 7 - LONE PINE CEMETERY (20.6 KM)

Direction to the stand. Return to the main road and follow the stick map south to Brighton Beach. Turn left and follow the signs to Kemalyeri or Conkbayiri. As your car's odometer approaches 19 kilometres you will notice a statue of a Turkish soldier carrying a wounded Anzac. At around 20.5 kilometres you will drive around a left-hand bend. Immediately after the bend, look for the signs to the Lone Pine Cemetery on the left. Walk up to the base of the large memorial tower and look towards the cemetery.

Lone Pine Memorial.

The terrain. The Turks called this area *Kanlisirt*, or Bloody Ridge. The Anzacs named it after a single, stunted pine tree that grew amongst the scrub, and a popular song of the time, 'The Trail of the Lonesome Pine'. Lone Pine represents the south-eastern point of the Anzac position and, due to the extent of the Australian casualties suffered here, is the principal Australian memorial on the battlefield. Where you are now standing was, until the August offensive, the approximate location of the Turkish front line. The Australian trenches were located towards the opposite end of the cemetery (west). During the period 6 to 10 August 1915, this area saw some of the bloodiest fighting of the campaign as the Australians struggled to hold the Turkish trench-line captured on the afternoon of 6 August.

Look along the road to your north. The road runs along the strategically vital Second Ridge, which marked the front line for most of the campaign. About a kilometre away you will notice a cream-coloured tower with a Turkish flag alongside. This marks the location of the Turkish *57th Regiment* Memorial (Stand 10). Just to the north of the Turkish memorial is a track off to the left (west) that takes you to The Nek (Stand 11). From the *57th Regiment* Memorial, the road runs north-east along the ridge through Baby 700 (Stand 12b) and up to Chunuk Bair (Stand 13). On a clear day you will notice a light-coloured brick monument on the skyline with a flag flying. This marks Chunuk Bair. From where you are now standing, to just north of the *57th Regiment* Memorial, the road represents what was no man's land, with the Australian positions on the western side of the road and the Turkish trench-lines on the eastern side.

Now look due east. The road runs away from you and disappears as it follows the Second Ridge down to Gaba Tepe. The ridge about a kilometre to your east is Third Ridge, or Gun Ridge—so named because it was a common location for Turkish artillery. The valley between you and Gun Ridge is Legge Valley. To your half left along Gun Ridge you will notice a white monument. This is the *Kemalyeri,* or 'Kemal's Place', known as Scrubby Knoll to the Anzacs. The Turkish commander, Kemal, had his headquarters near this knoll early in the campaign.

Looking south you begin to realise why Lone Pine was of strategic importance to both sides. From here you can see clearly all the way down to Gaba Tepe, along Brighton Beach and the approaches up Second Ridge from the south. This was one of the key pieces of terrain to the Anzacs. Had this position fallen, the Turks could have accessed the rear of the Anzac position and destroyed all the posts along Second Ridge.

What happened here?

First Battle for Lone Pine. Elements of the Anzac Covering Force arrived at Lone Pine at around 7.00 a.m. on the first day and attempted to locate a Turkish battery that was firing from this area. As they approached, the Turkish gun crews limbered up their guns and withdrew to the relative safety of Third Ridge (Gun Ridge). By mid-morning a number of Australians from the 6th Battalion and small groups from other battalions had pushed further south and south-east beyond Lone Pine and along Pine Ridge. Others had moved even further and were attempting to reach Gun Ridge by crossing Legge Valley. Many of these men were isolated and killed when the Turkish *27th Regiment* counter-attacked. Charles Bean, found many of the bodies when he returned in 1919.

Around 10.00 a.m. the Turks launched their first major counter-attack. Lieutenant Colonel Aker's *27th Regiment* had the task of dislodging the Australians from their positions along Second Ridge in the vicinity of Lone Pine and Johnston's Jolly (Stand 8). His aim was to secure the dominant 400 Plateau which was situated just behind Lone Pine. If he could achieve this, he could threaten the entire Anzac position. As his troops attacked north-west and west from Gun Ridge towards Lone Pine, he initially met resistance from small pockets of Australians who were crossing Legge Valley. This resistance was quickly overcome. Many of the Australians were killed while a few managed to withdraw back to Pine Ridge. Soon the Turks reached Pine Ridge and a short but bloody battle ensued. Some of the Australians made it back to the stronger positions near Lone Pine and

Johnston's Jolly (Stand 8), but most were killed. The Turks were in no mood to take prisoners that morning.

Late in the afternoon, Aker's *27th Regiment* was reinforced by the arrival of the *77th Regiment* and he immediately sent them into the fight. The fighting around Lone Pine and along Second Ridge was terrible: intense, bloody, hand-to-hand combat. One soldier later wrote:

Men stumbled and fell. The thump of bullets hitting muscle and bone was sickening, heard for the first time by most. It was if a giant scythe had swept across the field as men were cut down. To make matters worse, just then Abdul opened up with shrapnel.

In the end the Australians, now reinforced by the Kiwis, were only just able to hold on.

Lone Pine Memorial Wall.

August offensive. By August 1915, while the area around Lone Pine had been fought over almost continuously since the landing, neither side had been able to make any gains. It was the same story across the entire front. Static trench warfare had become the norm. In an attempt to break this deadlock, a major Anzac offensive was planned for August. Two fresh British divisions were landed at Suvla Bay, about 8 kilometres north of the Anzac positions, on 6 and 7 August. The primary objective of the offensive was the capture of the heights (Chunuk Bair (Stand 13), Hill Q and Hill 971). These high points were the vital ground in the Anzac sector and their capture was key to Hamilton's plan to finally break the deadlock. Several support attacks were planned along the entire Allied front, designed to tie up the Turk, have them commit their reinforcements and to capture ground. One of these attacks was planned for Lone Pine.

Around 2.00 p.m. on 6 August, three mines were exploded in tunnels under no man's land. These tunnels had been dug by the Australians in an effort to create some cover for the attack later that day by exploding mines to cause a cratered landscape. At 5.30 p.m., after a preliminary bombardment and with the setting sun in the enemy's eyes, Australians from the 1st Brigade (the 1st, 2nd, 3rd and 4th battalions) charged the Turkish trenches located at the eastern end of the current memorial. Most of the Turks, surprised by the intensity of the barrage, had moved back from the front line. The Australians were also in for a surprise. The forward trench they had attacked was not open but covered in logs and sand. While some troops hastily dug into the revetment, other Australians quickly moved along the rear of the Turkish position and entered the open communications trenches. As the battalions consolidated their positions, the engineers dug a connecting trench to protect the reinforcements now moving forward. By dark the Australians thought they had won an easy victory. But the battle was by no means over.

All through the night the Turks proved as committed to retaking their trenches as the Australians were to staying put. One member of the 1st Battalion, Private John Gammage, remembered that the 'bodies of both Turks and Anzacs were piled up 3 and 4 deep … the bombs simply poured in but as fast as our men went down another would take his place.' Another described the frenzied feeling that overtook the men, 'we felt like wild beasts'. Perhaps one of the best descriptions of both the preparation for, and the conduct of, the battle is provided by Private Richard Bulkeley of the 3rd Battalion:

Some time before 2pm, having sharpened our bayonets, dropped our packs and had a feed of bully beef, we moved into the line alongside 2 Bn. At 4.30pm the bombardment started and make no mistake, they did tear into it. The ground shook like a young earthquake and I was hoping the gunners wouldn't drop one short. The order came down the line : "Fix bayonets & stand by." As soon as the shelling stopped there were three short, sharp whistles – the signal to charge.

We were all up and out in a second and going for our lives. I saw men go down on either side of me, bullets whistled past my ears and chipped up the ground all around me but in no time I was with a mob of others in the first line of trenches and blazing away at the Turks. When they were all dead or cleared we jumped over the first line or ran over the overhead cover and on to the second line, and did the same thing there. All this time the Turks in the trenches on our left across Owens Gully were putting a hail of bullets on us from machine guns and rifles and about this time the Turkish artillery a mile away on our left began to pour shrapnel on us.

I was blazing away when I felt something hit my left hand – shrapnel or a bullet had cut the palm to the bone. When I tried to fire my rifle the whole arm seemed numb and useless, but not painful. I sat down and got out my field dressing to tie it up. Another fellow helped as I couldn't tie

the ends. Just as he finished he got a bullet through the foot. As I tried to tend to him he got another through his head. One of our machine guns had just set up beside us and opened up. I quickly moved out of its way when a shell burst just where I had been killing the three men working it.

Lieutenant Richard Bulkeley, 3rd Battalion. Private Bulkeley was evacuated to Egypt where he convalesced, eventually returning to Gallipoli in November and 'given a stripe'. After the evacuation he completed an officers' course in Egypt and was commissioned in early 1916. He was killed at Pozieres, France, in August 1916.

While we were fighting our engineers had been busy digging a quick trench across no man's land to join us to our lines. All the boys around me were now preparing for the inevitable counter attack – riveting the opposite side of the trench, shoring up collapsed areas, blocking off access to the Turks.

It was bloody, bloody business. While I couldn't use my rifle I busied myself collecting ammo from dead and wounded and taking it down the line. Where I could I helped by tying up the wounded. The Turks didn't let up all with bomb and grenade, but late evening our reinforcements had come over with supplies and bombs and we eventually got the upper hand. I was then told to move back with the wounded to the Bn dressing station, and eventually to the beach where I was evacuated.

By morning the Australians remained in place, but the Turks continued to attack. Bayonet, bomb, rifle, pistol, even brass knuckles and fists, were used in three days and nights of close-quarter fighting. The wounded and dead piled up and the pleas of the wounded were ignored. It was a desperate fight for survival. After three nights it was over. The Australians remained in possession of the trench but at a cost of over 2,000 casualties. The Turks had lost around 6,000. Some Australian battalions were virtually wiped out. The 3rd Battalion alone lost twenty-one of its twenty-three officers and two-thirds of its men. Seven Victoria Crosses were awarded to Australians at Lone Pine, testament to the ferocity of the fighting.

Things to see. Walk to the Lone Pine Memorial Wall. This is the main Australian memorial at Anzac and commemorates nearly 5,000 Australian and New Zealand servicemen who died in the Anzac area during the short eight-month campaign and whose graves are not known. Others named on the memorial died of wounds or illness and were buried in the waters off Gallipoli. Walk up to Panels 5 to 10. Listed here are the men from the 8th and 10th Light Horse Regiments who died in the ill-fated attack at The Nek (Stand 11).

The cemetery is partly located on the actual site of the Turkish trenches that were bloodily contested in the August offensive. Wander into the cemetery and locate the headstone of Private Hughie O'Donnell, 11th Battalion (8th row on right as you enter the cemetery, Plot I.G.15). Hughie was one of the youngest to fight at Gallipoli, and was only 16 years old when he was killed in action at Lone Pine on 12 May. His epitaph reads, 'He sleeps where Anzac heroes came to do and die.' Another is Private David Smith, 2nd Battalion (Plot II.D.8) who was killed on 27 May aged 17. The youngest soldier known to have fought at Gallipoli was Private James Martin who enlisted at 14. He died of fever on 25 October and was buried at sea. His name is listed on Panel 65. Also buried here are fifty-one Australians who were killed on 25 April 1915. Note that the headstones here do not actually match the location of the body. The men were buried unevenly, so when you are walking on the lawn areas you are most likely walking over the grave of one of these men.

OPTIONAL WALK 7A – OLD TRENCH-LINES

Duration: 30 mins **Difficulty:** Easy. Well defined track.

Walk through the cemetery to the southern side where you will find a track leading to your right (towards the sea). Walk along this track, which follows Bolton's and Holly Ridges. Bolton's Ridge represented the south-eastern sector of the Anzac front line. Holly Ridge, which spurs off Bolton's (and is the route taken by the fire trail you are on) contained a number of forward Australian posts. To the left and right of the track are numerous other small paths. Follow these and you are bound to come across depressions where the various forward and communications trenches ran. From some of these positions you will see the vista as viewed by both Australians and Turks in 1915, and can appreciate why this was such a strategically important location. Sometimes you can make amazing discoveries around these trenches—pieces of shrapnel, .303 rifle casings, bits of webbing and even skeletal remains.

View south towards Gaba Tepe from Lone Pine.

Evidence of the trauma of war is not difficult to find once you leave the main tracks.

Warning! It is illegal to remove any artefact from the Gallipoli battlefield. The entire battlefield is considered a cemetery where thousands of bodies remain buried in unknown graves.

OPTIONAL WALK 7B – DIGGERS' WALK TO SHELL GREEN

Duration: 15 mins one-way.
Distance: 1 km. **Difficulty:** Easy-medium. Well defined track, gradual descent to Shell Green.

This is the reverse of Optional Walk 6a and follows the old Artillery Road to Shell Green. There are amazing views along this route which is accessed on the left, just north of the Lone Pine Cemetery. Remember, unless you have a vehicle parked near Shell Green you will have to walk back up to Lone Pine.

STAND 8 - JOHNSTON'S JOLLY (20.9 KM)

Direction to the stand. After you have finished at Lone Pine, wander about 300 metres further north along the main road until you come to Johnston's Jolly on the right.

The terrain. Walk north along the road a few metres until you can see the course of the road as it runs up Second Ridge to your front. From here, depending on the thickness of the undergrowth, you should just make out the white memorial stones on the left of Courtney's and Steele's Post and Quinn's Post Cemeteries, and the monument tower at the Turkish *57th Regiment* Memorial. Looking east and south-east, the land drops away into Legge Valley and rises again onto Gun Ridge. To the south you will notice the Lone Pine Memorial. Where you are standing was no man's land for most of the campaign. The Johnston's Jolly Cemetery actually lies over the Turkish front line. The Anzac forward trenches were immediately opposite (west).

What happened here? Johnston's Jolly is named after Colonel George Johnston, Commander of the 2nd Field Artillery Brigade. Frustrated at his inability to counter the Turkish batteries, Johnston stated that if he had howitzers instead of the lighter field artillery he could 'jolly up' the

Turks in this area. Johnston's Jolly was initially occupied by scattered parties from the 2nd and 3rd Brigades on the first day of the campaign. Some of these parties ventured further east into Legge Valley and even onto Gun Ridge, before being repelled or killed by the Turkish counter-attack later that day. Others took cover on the 400 Plateau, including right here at Johnston's Jolly. Early in the afternoon of 25 April, Private George Mitchell of the 10th Battalion, and a group of mates, were taking cover from Turkish artillery in this vicinity and, 'mightily sick of being shelled', they:

Australian forward trench-line opposite Johnston's Jolly.

charge about 40yds over the crest and down into the bushes. Alex is hit in the stomach and all day he begged to be shot. We settle into a duel with the Turks a bit away but there are too many of them, and our cover isn't good. I heard a mushy thud and looking over saw that Crowther had had his face fearfully smashed in by a bullet. There was nothing I could do for him but pray that he might die swiftly.

In 1919, when the Johnston's Jolly Cemetery was established, the sun-bleached bones of Australians were found scattered in the valleys and gullies to the east of the road. By the end of the first day, the area to the east of the road was firmly in Turkish hands and remained so for the rest of the campaign.

Turkish May offensive. After the major Turkish counter-offensive of 19 May, Charles Bean wrote that:

On the night of 17 May, someone tapped into our telephone line & tapped out a message 'We will put you in the sea tomorrow you Australian bastards. Big guns we will give you, and big mines, you Australian bastards.' The day of the 18th was unusually quiet. Our aeroplane has spotted a Turk division unloading behind Maidos. We all expected an attack any time.

The attack came at 3.20 a.m. on 19 May across the Turks entire front. Johnson's Jolly was the left of the Turkish attack, with Quinn's and Pope's Posts in the centre. Approximately 42,000 Turks attacked a vastly inferior force of 12,500 Australians and New Zealanders. Despite their superior numbers, the Turkish attack was blighted by poor secrecy, intelligence and planning. Their build-up was detected by an observation plane from the Royal Naval Air Service, giving the Anzacs plenty of time to prepare, and they lacked sufficient artillery ammunition to properly support their infantry. The clear night also enabled lookouts at Johnston's Jolly to spot a large force moving towards Steele's Post (about 150 metres north of Johnston's Jolly) at around 3.00 a.m. The Anzacs were ready and waiting for them.

Bean wrote that:

Our men had been Standing To since 3am in expectation of an attack. They seemed to come at us across their entire line at the same time. They didn't appear well trained as there was no attempt at covering fire so our men could sit on the parapet and shoot for all they were worth. They made two charges, but near 4th Bn (to our right) they made four. And at Quinns five or six.

For the Turkish infantrymen it was akin to suicide. Australians likened defending against the wild, reckless charges of the Turks to a 'wallaby drive'. Men were firing at the Turks as fast as they could reload. Barrels glowed red hot. Over 948,000 rifle and machine-gun rounds were fired by the Australians alone. Australians in reserve positions ignored orders and pushed forward into the firing line 'to get a crack at the Turk'. Some

men actually paid for a position in the forward trench or fought with one another for a better position. By mid-morning 'the dead and wounded lay everywhere in the hundreds.' Turkish casualties were around 10,000. Anzac casualties were comparatively light at about 600.

Private Bulkeley, whose battalion was located opposite Johnston's Jolly when the Turks attacked, provided a graphic description of events in his diary:

Went into the firing line at 6pm. Turks have been heavily reinforced and word is they'll attack us tonight. I had a good posy and spent the first watch getting ready – filled an empty biscuit tin with dirt so I could stand on it when the rush came and shoot over the parapet. Cleaned out about 100 rounds of ammo in clips and had them lined up between sand bags so I could get to them quickly.

About half hour before dawn they attacked. Could only see dark forms, but our company put up a deadly hail of fire. As it grew light we could see them plainly and better aim our shots. You couldn't miss at 15 or so yards as they came is swarms. Hundreds of them at a time. Our machine guns mowed down thousands. My rifle got so hot that the bolt kept sticking and I had to keep spitting on it to get it to work. After a while someone down in the trench handed me another rifle. I used up two others before it was over.

Gradually the attack started to die out and those that were left tried to get back to their lines, but few made it – our boys are too good shots for that. Quite a few of our own lads also got hit. They made the mistake of staying up on their parapets as things died down and the snipers got them. Our company lost 36 that morning – most shot through the head. Lieutenant Stutsbury was shot through the mouth and Lieutenant Burleigh through the stomach and later died.

Turkish dead after the disastrous attack on 19 May. *(AWM A05614)*

With the onset of summer, both sides were concerned at the health risk posed by the large number of rotting corpses lying exposed in no man's land. The day after the attack was one of the hottest since the landing. Bodies started to bloat and flies descended on the corpses. With the flies came disease and illness which

attacked both sides. A ceasefire was eventually arranged for 24 May. Both Turk and Anzac spent the entire day burying the dead on their side of the line. One Australian noted, 'the stench is sickening. The burial party has indeed a horrible job.' Another wrote home, 'no words can describe the ghastliness' of the burials. 'The bodies were horrible to look at being black and swelled up stretching out the clothing and, in many cases, when they were touched, falling to pieces.'

Many officers took the chance to dress as ordinary soldiers and collect any intelligence they could. According to a popular rumour even Mustafa Kemal participated in this charade. The Anzacs came face to face with their enemy under less bloodcurdling circumstances and they saw that the Turk was just another soldier doing his duty. Numerous letters home afterwards displayed admiration for the enemy. Men swapped food and cigarettes and a form of camaraderie was soon apparent. After this attack a mutual respect developed between Turk and Anzac.

Things to see. Move to the west side of the road and climb into one of the old Australian trench-lines that remains exposed here. The wooden trench supports have long since rotted away but it is easy to see the line of the forward Australian trenches. The first trench off the road runs north-south. This was the Australian front-line trench. Behind the forward trench are other trenches that run parallel to the forward trench. These were reserve or support trenches that gave the position depth and could hold reserve troops. These trench-lines were connected by communications trenches that ran east-west from the forward-most trench to the rear areas. As the Turks had a similar trench design, the Anzac Peninsula in 1915 was a maze of trenches, tunnels and dugouts.

An Australian trench. Note the man asleep in the cut-out behind Captain Fry. *(AWM A05401)*

It was impossible to bury the dead properly in these front-line positions, and the smell of rotting flesh together with the threat of disease, made it imperative that the bodies be covered in some way. Consequently, both the Australian and Turkish forward trenches incorporated the corpses of their own men and those of the enemy and it was not uncommon for there to be grisly reminders in the form of exposed body parts poking into the trench.

Troops lived in these trenches for months at a time with only occasional relief from the stress, strain, monotony and danger. Conditions were atrocious. Men suffered from septic sores, lice and plagues of flies, and endured the terrible smells of open latrines and rotting corpses. In summer they were exposed to the harsh sun and suffered constant thirst while, in winter, they lived in rain, mud and snow. One man wrote that in summer men 'learned to curse the sun as an enemy more cruel than the Turk. With the sun and the plague of flies came the torment of thirst.' Another recorded, 'You ought to see the Anzac fleas, millions of them, and other things that crawl and stick closer than a brother. My blanket nearly walks by itself.' One entry in the war diary of the 12th Infantry Brigade in September notes that:

The general health is bad with as many as 50 per cent of the men unfit for duty and unless relieved there will be, to a certainty, a severe epidemic of pneumonia, dysentery and enteric fever as the resisting power to disease is practically nil.

Walk behind the Australian trenches near the road. Here you can still see the old communications trenches that supported the front line. Some of these run all the way back to the 400 Plateau. From here (the 400 Plateau) you will have an extensive view of the ridgeline running from MacLagan's Ridge, through Plugge's Plateau, the Razor Edge, on and across Russell's Top and on to The Nek. This finger ridgeline was key terrain at Anzac, and from this position you gain a true appreciation of its importance.

Sign to 4th Battalion Parade Ground Cemetery.

OPTIONAL WALK 8A - 4TH BATTALION PARADE GROUND CEMETERY (21.1KM)

Duration: 10 min one-way.
Distance: 200 m from road.
Difficulty: Easy, but a steep ascent back to the road.

About 200 metres along the road from Johnston's Jolly you will come to a short track off to the left and signed to the 4th Battalion Parade Ground Cemetery (you have gone too far if you come to Courtney's and Steele's Post Cemetery). The track is about 300 metres long and quite steep in places. However, it is a well-maintained track and, from this cemetery, you can wander over Braund's Hill, a finger feature that extends west towards Ari Burnu and the coast. Braund's Hill affords great views down Shrapnel Valley, Bridges' Road and the rear of Second Ridge (the Anzac front line). From here you can clearly appreciate the importance of the Posts on the ridge above you. Had they fallen, the Turks would have had relatively easy passage all the way to the beach. For part of the campaign the 4th Battalion manned the forward trench-line that ran from just north of Johnston's Jolly up towards Steele's Post. Buried here are two men the Official Historian, Charles Bean, regarded as the among the best commanders at Gallipoli: Colonel Henry MacLaurin (Plot A.10), who commanded the 1st Brigade, and Lieutenant Colonel Astley Onslow Thompson (Plot A.11), Commander of the 4th Battalion. MacLaurin was shot and killed by a Turkish sniper on 28 April while warning others to stay under cover. Onslow Thompson died on 26 April leading his battalion in an attack across Lone Pine. The graves of both of these men are immediately in front of you as you walk into the 4th Battalion Parade Ground cemetery.

As you follow the path back up to the road, watch for a narrow track on your left just before the summit. This track will take you behind Steele's Post where the remains of several dugouts can still be seen. Exercise caution as the area is steep and the ground unstable in places.

View down Shrapnel Valley from Braund's Hill. Shrapnel Valley Cemetery is visible in the background with Plugge's Plateau rising to the far right.

OPTIONAL WALK 8B - COURTNEY'S AND STEELE'S POST CEMETERY (21.2KM)

Duration: 10 mins one-way.
Distance: 300 m from Johnston's Jolly. **Difficulty:** Easy.

About 300 metres north along the road from Johnston's Jolly, or just a short walk from the entrance track to the 4th Battalion Parade Ground Cemetery, is Courtney's and Steele's

Post Cemetery. Steele's Post is named after Major Steele of the 14th Battalion, with Courtney's Post taking its name from Lieutenant Colonel Courtney, Commanding Officer of the 14th Battalion. Steele's Post was located near where the 4th Battalion Parade Ground track meets the main road, extending south to the northern end of Braund's Hill. Courtney's Post is a short walk further north (about 100 metres) and was the centre of the three main posts (Steele's, Courtney's and Quinn's) that constituted the Anzac eastern front. The 11th Battalion captured this ground on 25 April, with the 14th Battalion arriving on the 27th. The post held out against ferocious Turkish counter-attacks in late April and during the Turkish offensive in late May. The cemetery was erected on the old trenches of Steele's Post in 1919, with the eastern side of the cemetery representing the Australian front line. The Turkish trenches were only a few metres away on the opposite side of the road. In the area behind the Australian trenches was a shanty town of dugouts and shelters, much of it this now eroded over time. Private Albert Jacka, 22 years of age, won Australia's first Victoria Cross in this area on 19 May while with the 14th Battalion. During the major Turkish offensive on this date, a section of Courtney's Post was occupied by a party of Turks. Taking the initiative, Jacka 'dove in amongst them shooting five, bayoneting two and forcing the rest to flee.'

Private Bulkeley was stationed near here with the 3rd Battalion for much of his stay at Anzac. In his diary he gives an account of the daily life of a soldier at Gallipoli;

Each of the battalions have four companies [sic], each with four platoons. With each platoon having four sections. I'm in 9 platoon, C company, and our company's firing line took [up an area] about 120m … During the day we had one platoon in the firing line, one in support in the main communications trench, one in reserve in the support trenches, and one resting. At night there were two platoons in the firing line, one in support and one in reserve. You generally move in [a] circle so, 9 platoon will go from the communications trench to the firing line tonight. After a 6 hour stretch we'll then probably move back into the rest trenches. But there's never much rest. Always water to cart, a trench to dig or repair, lines to mend, etc.

It's a well-worn routine. Our sgt warns us out to move about 5.30pm. We then clean our rifle and get ready. At 6pm we move into the line in full kit – loaded rifle, 200 rounds of ammo, and bayonet fixed. We'll be in the line until midnight. Every

third posy has an observation station and each posy usually holds two men. You go on watch into the observation station in pairs and do one hour on and two off. At night both of us must observe. When dark you have to observe over the top of the sand bags. A common dodge on both sides is to train a machine gun on your observation post before dark then snipe away at you all night. Every night you get casualties.

After an hour of observing you and your mate try and sleep in the bottom of the trench until you're called again. It's a buggar trying to sleep with people moving about all night in a narrow, dark trench – you get stood on all the time. Just as you drop off to sleep you'll get kicked in the ribs by the sgt for Stand To. It was standard British army practice to Stand To from a half-hour before dawn till a half-hour after. You can't image how much we all hated Stand To.

At midnight we move back to the support trenches, but we are on again at 6am. During the day we are the only platoon from our company in the line and you have to observe using a periscope, doing 2 hours on and four off. In the day only one has to observe with the other cleaning up a bit, yarning, smoking, reading and sniping a bit.

At midday we move into the support trenches again and stay there all afternoon and night. These trenches are lined on either side with sleeping bays about 6' x 2'. But you have to keep your kit on and rifle handy. The following morning at 6am we moved further back for a rest and remained there all day. There wasn't much to do so we got permission for a swim and to trade with the navy coves to supplement our rations —you sure tire of bully beef and biscuits.

Just past cemetery, follow dirt road on right for about 500 metres, signposted *Cataldere Sehitligi*. This is a mass Turk grave containing nearly 3,000 bodies and it provides excellent views of the rear of the Turk's lines.

STAND 9 - QUINN'S POST (21.6 KM)

Direction to the stand. Quinn's Post is approximately 800 metres from Johnston's Jolly, or 400 metres from Courtney's and Steele's Post Cemetery. Follow the road north and watch for the sign on the left-hand side of the road. Stand on a high point at the north-west corner of the cemetery and face west, towards the ocean.

Quinn's Post Cemetery with the Turkish *57th Regiment* Memorial in the background.

The terrain. From here you should be looking directly at the top of Plugge's Plateau, with the entrance to Shrapnel Valley (and, on a clear day, Shrapnel Valley Cemetery) to the left of Plugge's Plateau and Russell's Top to the right. You can also see the course of Shrapnel and Monash Valleys, the latter running right up to just below your position. Monash Valley carried the lifeblood of supplies to Quinn's Post and other parts of the Anzac front line.

Facing north you can see the *57th Regiment* Memorial tower and Turkish flag. About a hand's width to the left of the tower, where you see a copse of trees on the horizon, is The Nek. Further to the left of The Nek (north-west) you should be able to make out Pope's Post. Both Pope's Post and Russell's Top provided depth to this section of the Anzac line and their machine-guns were sited to support Quinn's Post with deadly accuracy.

At the head of Monash Valley, where it cuts between Quinn's and Pope's Posts, are Bloody Angle and Dead Man's Ridge. Many Anzac lives were lost around these two positions in attacks and counter-attacks against the Turks. The dominating hill just to the north of the *57th Regiment* Memorial is Baby 700. This hill was occupied by the Turks for most of the campaign and, while observation is affected by the scrubby vegetation today, at that time the enemy enjoyed excellent observation and fields of fire onto Quinn's Post. Running south from Baby 700 is Mortar Ridge. This ridge was also in enemy hands and well within range of rifle fire.

Looking to the east you can see Third Ridge (Gun, Ridge). Visible is the *Kemalyeri* Turkish Monolith on Scrubby Knoll (about one kilometre distant), where Colonel Kemal had his headquarters for a time. Where you are now standing was the northern section of Quinn's Post, with the cemetery built over some of the old tunnels on Quinn's Post. The main position is about 100 metres to the south. Further south was Courtney's Post. Sections of Quinn's and Courtney's Posts could provide mutually supporting fire, saving these posts from being overrun on several occasions.

What happened here? Quinn's Post was the scene of some of the most ferocious and relentless fighting in the campaign. With the enemy so close, the post was subjected to constant bombing (hand-grenade) attacks. Indeed, the Turks called this area *Bomba Sirt* because of the ceaseless bombing. In late April the Queensland 15th Battalion moved into this section of the front line and garrisoned Quinn's Post throughout May. The position was named after an officer of that battalion, Major Hugh Quinn, who was killed in action on 29 May 1915, at the age of 27. He is buried in the Shrapnel Valley Cemetery. Four of the five officers in Quinn's Charlie Company were killed at the post during May, with the fifth officer severely wounded. Overall, the 15th Battalion lost eight officers and 350 men in its first week at Quinn's Post, a casualty rate of more than a third.

Captain Quinn, 15th Battalion. *(AWM H17420)*

In June, with the arrival of Lieutenant Colonel William Malone and his New Zealand Wellington Battalion, Quinn's Post received a much needed upgrade. Trenches were deepened and parapets strengthened. Wire nets were erected to catch the bombs and men were trained in the use of the new periscope rifle. Malone's aim was to fortify Quinn's Post and establish fire supremacy over the Turk. These changes were long overdue and had an almost immediate impact. Casualty rates at Quinn's Post dropped, as did enemy sniping and bombing.

Despite these improvements, the danger at Quinn's Post was ever-present and the tension felt by the troops who manned the post unremitting over the course of the entire campaign. The men were never safe as the post was either actually under attack or about to be attacked. So great was the trauma of this place that men 'looked upon it as they would a haunted house'. Over the period of the campaign about 3,000 men served at Quinn's Post. Hundreds of them lie here still. Sticking one's head above the parapet meant almost certain death as the Turks occupied the higher ground. The invention of the periscope rifle in May by Lance Corporal Beech of the 2nd Battalion allowed the Australians to fire back without the firer exposing himself to the ever-ready Turkish

riflemen overlooking Quinn's Post. So effective was this periscope that, by June, Turkish sniping was suppressed to the extent that Monash Valley could be traversed in relative safety during daylight. Even captured Turks praised the Anzacs' marksmanship.

Periscope rifles in use at Quinn's Post. *(Artwork by Jeff Isaacs)*

Anzac's first offensive. Anzac's first offensive was launched from Quinn's Post on 2 May when Major General Godley's NZ&A Division launched an attack to retake Baby 700 (north-east of Quinn's Post). The Australian 4th Infantry Brigade, under the command of the then Colonel Monash, attacked from Quinn's Post but the enemy was too well entrenched and the attack failed with over 1,000 Anzac casualties. A week later Godley ordered the 15th Battalion at Quinn's Post to attack the enemy's trenches opposite, despite intelligence that the line was strongly held. At 10.45 p.m. on 9 May, 100 men from the 15th Battalion attacked. Despite some initial successes, the

Turks launched a massive counter-attack which forced the 16th Battalion to come to the rescue of the 15th. By dawn on 10 May, the Australians had been forced to retire to their original trenches, leaving over 200 of their mates behind.

With these losses, and disaster at Helles which consumed two Anzac brigades, Birdwood ordered the 1st Australian Light Horse Brigade and the New Zealand Mounted Brigade—without their horses—to Gallipoli from Egypt. Elements of Colonel Harry Chauvel's 1st Light Horse Brigade were employed here at Quinn's Post soon after their arrival. Within hours there were casualties, partly due to the inadequacy of their training in Egypt and the extreme dangers at Quinn's Post.

Tunneling. The Turks were eager to take Quinn's Post as they realised that if they occupied this area the Anzacs would find it very difficult to reinforce and supply other units on the front line. In the aftermath of their disastrous attack on 19 May, they attempted to capture the area by different means, tunneling under no man's land and exploding a mine under Quinn's Post. While their initial attempts failed, they were not deterred and, at 3.20 a.m. on 29 May, a large explosion 'shook the valley' killing eleven men from the 13th Battalion. The Turks had exploded a mine directly in front of Quinn's Post and, before the dust had settled, launched an attack. While the attack failed, it proved the value of tunneling and, for the rest of the campaign, both sides used it extensively; the Anzacs forming specialist tunneling companies populated by men with mining experience. It was dangerous work. Many of the tunnelers were killed in cave-ins or counter-mining explosions planted by the Turks. Tunneling at Quinn's Post was particularly dangerous. Half of the 28-strong New Zealand sappers sent to work around Quinn's Post were killed within six days.

Dugouts behind Quinn's Post. The area along the Second Ridge looked more like a mining camp than a war zone. *(AWM A02009)*

Things to see. Quinn's Post is one of the easiest locations to visit to develop a sense of what it must have been like to have lived and fought at Gallipoli. Take a wander through what was the Australian front line, then follow the cemetery's south wall until you arrive at the edge of Monash Valley. From here there is a clear view down Monash Valley. Carefully climb down the side of the hill a few metres until you arrive at one of the old terraces. All around you were living areas, dugouts, accommodation tents, stores, ammunition and a first aid post.

Now walk over to the road. The Australian positions were on the western side of the road and the Turkish trenches on the eastern. The road itself runs through what was no man's land. For large sections of this front the two sides were only about twenty metres apart. As you walk around the area it is still possible to see where many of these trenches were. On the Turkish side of the road you can clearly see their old trench-line. The slope behind their trenches is much gentler here, and the area was hidden from Anzac observation. This permitted a much easier passage of supplies and reinforcements for the Turks than that endured by the Anzacs.

The cemetery holds the remains of or commemorates 473 men, most unidentified. In addition, special memorials record the names of 64 soldiers, most of them Australian,

who were known or believed to have been buried in this area. Notice the battalions to which the men belonged. The cemetery provides a list of the units that fought and died here: 13th, 14th, 15th and 16th Battalions, 1st and 2nd Light Horse Regiments, the Otago Regiment and the British Portsmouth Battalion. The front row of headstones (closest to the memorial cross) marks those 15th Battalion men killed in the first week of fighting.

STAND 10 - TURKISH 57TH REGIMENT MEMORIAL (21.8 KM)

Direction to the stand. Leave Quinn's Post and, about 200 metres further along the main road on the left, is a parking area, some stalls and a toilet. On the opposite side of the road is the 57th Regiment Memorial (*57. Alay Sehitligi ve Aniti*). In the car park area is a large statue of a Turkish soldier, *Turk Askerine Saygi* (Respect for the Turkish Soldier). Note that his rifle is actually a British .303 Lee Enfield. The Turks were desperately low on ammunition in the early days of the campaign and would often swap their own rifles for those of dead Anzacs who usually carried around 60 rounds of ammunition (the British rimmed .303-inch ammunition did not fit the Mauser Model 1893 rifle used by the Turkish Army).

Mehmet (Turkish soldier) statue outside the Turkish *57th Regiment* Memorial. *(photo by author)*

Walk to a high point behind the stalls (i.e. west) and find a position that gives you a view over the Anzac area.

What happened here? Initially the Anzacs underestimated their enemy. It was widely expected that the Turkish Army would simply run away at the sight of the Allied force massed against them. However, as the fighting in this area showed on 25 April and during their numerous clashes throughout the campaign, the Turkish soldier was as proficient a fighter as his Allied opponent. During the fighting in May both sides developed a deep respect for their enemy. The Anzacs were surprised to find in the *Mehmets* many

of the characteristics they took pride in themselves: courage, comradeship, proficiency and marksmanship, referring to them as 'bloody good shots'. Both sides even swapped gifts. The Official Historian, Charles Bean, describes this in one of his despatches:

... near daybreak one morning there came out of their trench at Quinn's a packet tied to a string, thrown so it lobbed near our parapet and lay outside between the trenches. Of course, our sentries waited for it to explode or fizz or burst into smoke or some such devilry. The sergeant near it looked at it very carefully through a telescope. ... Before the sergeant knew what was happening the man next him had climbed up on to the parapet and stepped round the netting and into the deadly area between the trenches and was bringing back the packet. It was a small packet of cigarettes. In it, scrawled in indelible pencil and in badly spelt French, were the words, 'A Notre Herox Ennemis' ('To our heroic enemies'). Of course some return had to be made, and so our men threw over a tin or two of bully beef. Presently back flew a piece of paper wrapped round a stone. It read 'Bully beef non.' After that we threw some sweet biscuits and a tin of jam. Other cigarettes came back [and a note saying] 'Envoyez Milk' ('Send us milk'). Then one of them waved

*down with his hands and shouted
'Fini'. And our men waved back, and
down gradually went the two lines of
smiling heads, and after a pause of a
minute or two the bombs began to fly
again. They had begun at half-past 8
and they lasted until about a quarter
past 9. The same courtesies repeated
themselves next morning.*

Turkish trenches were generally more substantial
and better constructed than those of the Anzacs.
(Artwork by Jeff Isaacs)

While the Anzacs were quick to
identify with the Turkish soldier,
there remained numerous differences.
Few of the Mehmets could read or
write, whereas most of the Anzacs
could. The Turkish soldier accepted
the orders of his leader uncondition-
ally and unquestioningly, whereas the
Australians in particular thought it
their right to 'ignore bloody stupid
orders'. One German officer described
the Mehmets under his command as
'contented, religious and modest'. A

British general portrayed the Australians as 'brash and brazen with a
propensity to blaspheme.'

There were differences in trench life,
too. The Australians were desperately
short of water in the summer, and
drenched with the onset of winter.
Partly for this reason the usual trench
diseases and ailments afflicted the
Anzacs throughout the campaign.
The Turks, however, generally had
a good supply of water, were used
to the climate and suffered less from
disease than the Anzacs. Many of the
Turkish trenches were also superior
to those of the Anzacs and included
overhead protection, drains and even
concrete steps. In addition, the Turk
diet of vegetables, rice, bread and oil
was far better for the overall health
of their soldiers than the Anzac diet
of bully beef and hard tack biscuits.
One soldier's description of his diet
highlights the monotony of Anzac
fare: 'In the morning we get a piece of
bacon, a pint of tea and hard biscuits,
perhaps a loaf of bread. For dinner, we
have water, tea and sugar, and for tea
we have bully beef stew.'

The Anzacs were surprised at the
marksmanship skills of the Turks.
Many of the Australians had only fired
a few dozen rounds with their Lee
Enfield .303 rifle before landing at
Gallipoli and took some time to 'get
their eye in'. The Turks, on the other

hand, impressed the Anzacs with their 'noticeable superiority in machine-gunnery' and their 'excellence in sniping'. The accuracy of the enemy snipers was such that officers were encouraged to 'carry a rifle and hide their field glasses', or risk being identified as an officer and, therefore, become the target of a Turkish sniper. Indeed, so many officers had been hit by Turkish snipers in the first few weeks of the campaign, including Generals Bridges and Birdwood, that the Anzac battalions formed counter-sniping teams.

Turkish sniper. The origins of this picture are uncertain and it may have been staged for the camera. Private Greenwood of the 8th Battalion wrote to his parents of one sniper whom 'you could not see in daytime he being exactly like a bush... He was getting a lot of our men all the time.' (AWM G00377)

Things to see. The Memorial was built in 1992 on the lower slope of Baby 700. In 1915 this position was referred to by the Anzacs as 'The Chessboard', due to the network of intersecting

enemy trenches that existed here. During the war the Allies buried their dead in temporary cemeteries. After the war the Commonwealth War Graves Commission relocated a number of these temporary cemeteries, buried numerous bodies that were not located until after the ceasefire and recorded the names of all those who had been interred. The Turks, on the other hand, did not establish cemeteries. Where you are now is a memorial park rather than a Turkish cemetery. What appear to be headstones are simply symbolic; there are very few actual graves here.

As you walk into the Memorial you will notice a statue of an old man and a child. In 1990, on the 75th anniversary of the landing, the Anzac Day ceremonies at Gallipoli were attended by numerous veterans from both sides. This statue is of Turkish Gallipoli veteran, *Huseyein Kacmaz*, who attended with his great-grand daughter. He died four years later, aged 110.

The plaques in the park display the names of soldiers of the *57th Regiment*. This regiment was the Anatolian Turkish regiment of Mustapha Kemal's *19th Division*. This was the first Turkish unit to resist the Anzac landing on 25 April 1915 and led the counter-attack on 25 April, finally retaking this position from the Anzacs after desperate fighting.

Charge at The Nek. George Lambert's painting of the 3rd Light Horse Brigade's charge at The Nek on 7 August 1915. *(AWM ART07965)*

STAND 11 - THE NEK (22 KM)

Direction to the stand. Just a short distance north from the *57th Regiment* Memorial, on the left, is a sign directing you to The Nek Cemetery. Walk or drive about 150 metres along this track until you come to the cemetery. On the south-western side of the cemetery are some reconstructed trenches on the site of the original trenches used by the Australian Light Horse.

The terrain. The Nek is actually a narrow saddle, only 30 metres wide, between Russell's Top and Baby 700. The name was most likely coined by veterans of the South African war, where it was used to describe a narrowing or gap between two hills. During the

Gallipoli campaign this area was devoid of trees, offering excellent fields of view and clear fire lanes to the Turks who occupied the higher ground to your front (the base of Baby 700), to your right (the present location of the *57th Regiment* Memorial), and even as far south as the high ground in front of Steele's Post (German Officers' Ridge). On the opposite side of the cemetery is a small Turkish memorial known as Sergeant Mehmet's tomb. This was the Turkish front line which had excellent depth due to the several other layers of enemy trenches and machine-gun posts extending up Baby 700 behind (see below photograph of The Nek taken in 1919). Today it is hard to see where these Turkish positions would have

143

been. Soon after the Allied landings this area was cleared of scrub and trees, providing the enemy with good observation and fields of fire on to the Australian forward trenches, which are in the area of where you are now standing. The cemetery to your front was no man's land for much of 1915.

What happened here? Australian infantry, mostly from the 11th and 12th Battalions, arrived at The Nek early on the first morning, some having crossed Russell's Top (Stand 12a) and others having climbed the almost sheer face near Walker's Ridge (Stand 12). Small groups moved past The Nek and secured Baby 700 (Stand 12b), the next feature, about 250 metres north-east of your current location. Some even pushed on further towards Chunuk Bair (Stand 13). Around 10.00 a.m., while

the Australians were attempting to secure their positions, Mustafa Kemal launched his first counter-attack. The Turkish *57th Regiment* attacked towards The Nek, overrunning those Australians who had attempted to capture Chunuk Bair. Some made it back to Baby 700. Many others were never seen again. A short time later, the positions on Baby 700 were also seriously threatened. The Australians on this feature were eventually forced back to The Nek, making it the north-eastern point of the Anzac front line.

The arrival of the Kiwis in the afternoon was greeted with much relief by the hard-pressed Australians at The Nek. They arrived just in time to strengthen the position against the expected Turkish counter-attack. At dusk the Turkish *3rd Battalion* of the *57th Regiment*, overconfident after

THE NEK & SURROUNDS

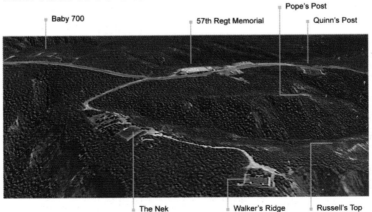

The Nek and surrounds
(Image by Mark Wahlert)

their easy victory in retaking Baby 700, launched their attack on The Nek. This time the Anzacs were ready, opening fire with machine-gun and rifle when the enemy was no more than 20 metres from their positions. The Turks were slaughtered and the attack evaporated in minutes.

The Charge at The Nek. This location is most famous for the attack depicted in Peter Weir's 1981 film, *Gallipoli*. From where you are now standing, men from the 8th and 10th Light Horse Regiments launched a courageous but doomed attack against well-defended Turkish positions only 30 metres to your front. The attack was part of the August offensive and was designed to support the main Anzac assault on the heights (Chunuk Bair, Hill Q and Hill 971). At 4.30 a.m. on 7 August, the first of four waves of men went over the top. The area was not large enough to allow one massive assault. Within 15 minutes, 234 Australian Light Horsemen were dead and 138 more wounded.

The assault at The Nek was only part of a complex and ambitious plan that involved similar attacks along the entire Anzac front line. These attacks were designed to eliminate Turkish machine-guns sited to the front and on the flanks at The Nek. Even more optimistic was the view that the supporting attacks would force the Turks facing The Nek, Colonel Kemal's *19th Infantry Division*, to withdraw. Unfortunately for the 3rd Light Horse Brigade, none of this occurred.

Old Anzac trench at The Nek.

The first indication of a flaw in the plan came with the failure of the preliminary attack to silence the Turkish machine-guns at German Officers' Trench (to the front of Steele's Post). Similar attacks from Quinn's and Pope's Posts also failed. However, of more immediate concern to the 8th Light Horse Regiment was the cessation of the supporting Allied artillery and naval barrage seven minutes prior to the commencement of their attack. This gave the Turks ample time to climb back into their trenches and man their machine-guns. Why the barrage ended early will never be known; probably a combination of poor staff work, the artillery and

Light Horse not having synchronised their watches and the gunners' fear of hitting their own men.

Nevertheless, at the appointed time of 4.30 a.m., the first wave of 150 men from the 8th Light Horse Regiment, led by their Commanding Officer, Lieutenant Colonel White, charged the well-defended and now ready and waiting Turkish trench-line. Within a few seconds most were killed or wounded. White made it all of ten yards before he was killed. All the officers in that first wave were hit.

Captain Hore, standing with his men ready in the second wave, wrote afterwards, 'We saw our fate in front of us, but … not a man in the second line stayed in his trench.' At 4.32 a.m., on the sound of a whistle blast, Hore and his men from the 8th Light Horse quickly climbed from their trench and charged. As with the first line, the second seemed to 'dissolve in a hail of Turkish bullets before our eyes'.

After the disaster of the first two waves, Colonel Brazier, Commanding Officer of the 10th Light Horse Regiment, harangued his brigade headquarters to stop the attack. Specifically, Brazier had a shouting match with his Brigade Major, Major Antill, an incident which is loosely portrayed in Peter Weir's film, *Gallipoli*. The argument concerned the apparent sighting of an Australian marker flag in the forward enemy trenches. It was common in the early days of trench warfare for the attacking force to carry marker flags to indicate to those following where there had been a breach of the enemy's fortifications, and for their artillery to see where friendly forces were located (thereby reducing the risk of 'friendly fire'). Antill used the report of such a marker flag to insist that the attack continue so as to support those men who might be fighting for their lives in the enemy's trenches. This remained a controversial issue for many years, as a number of those involved in the attack denied that any of the troops had even reached the enemy trench-line, let alone been able to post a marker flag. Following the war, the Commanding Officer of the Turkish *27th Regiment* at The Nek, *Sefik Bey*, published his account of the battle which confirmed that some Australians had penetrated a section of the *27th*'s trench, but had been quickly killed.

The third and fourth wave of men from the 10th Light Horse Regiment attacked the alert and waiting Turkish line and fared no better than their predecessors. Once the first wave had attacked, the men waiting to go in the subsequent waves knew that they were likely to die. There was little chatter; just the torrent of enemy gunfire, then silence. Hundreds were killed outright. Others slowly bled to death or were picked off by Turkish riflemen or bombers. Some men's legs were completely severed by machine-gun fire. A few, including Captain Hore, found some temporary shelter from the gunfire among the dead from the previous waves and lay still in the heat of the day waiting for nightfall to crawl back to their trenches.

The Nek, 1919. This picture was taken from the old Australian trenches looking towards Sergeant Mehmet's Tomb. At the time this picture was taken, during the Historical Mission to Gallipoli in 1919, the area in between these two points held the remains of over 300 bodies. Note the thigh bone in the foreground and scattered skeletal remains to the left. *(AWM P03631.228)*

The impact of the charge was felt by all those at Anzac. Many wrote home about the futility of charging the Turkish positions. One soldier who watched the survivors straggle into the first aid station recorded, 'It was a truly awful sight. Once more the long procession of wounded, dirty, ragged, torn and bloody men came down from The Nek to the dressing station while others lay just 25 yards [23 metres] in front of the trench in the hot sun . . .' The terrain—the narrow area of land between two steep valleys—and the strength of the Turkish positions there, made any attack futile. The Official Historian, Charles Bean, called the charge of the 3rd Light Horse Brigade 'one of the bravest actions in the history of war'. Many others considered it simply a waste of good men.

Things to see. Walk into the cemetery which is built on what was no man's land. In this small area 326 Australians lay dead or wounded on the morning of 7 August. Some of the wounded managed to crawl back to their comrades and were quickly pulled into the safety of the trenches. Others died where they fell and, for the rest of the campaign, lay exposed to the elements, as it was too dangerous to recover their bodies. In 1919, the Graves Registration Unit found and buried the unidentified remains of over 300 Australians.

Walk up to Sergeant Mehmet's Tomb, which marks the Turkish front line and the initial objective of the Australian Light Horse charge. Sergeant Mehmet fought and died near here on the first day of the fighting. Move further behind the tomb and notice the Turks' clear fields of fire into their killing zone (the area of the cemetery).

View south from Walker's Ridge looking down on Ari Burnu and North Beach. The profile of the Sphinx can be seen in the upper left.

STAND 12 - WALKER'S RIDGE

Direction to the stand. After you leave The Nek Cemetery, walk down the dirt road track that runs west (towards the ocean). A few hundred metres along you will come to the small Walker's Ridge Cemetery. The cemetery is named after Brigadier Walker who commanded the New Zealand Infantry Brigade and whose headquarters was located in this area. Walk into the cemetery.

The terrain. The view over Anzac from this point is magnificent, stretching as far as North Beach, where you commenced this tour. Be careful where you stand, as there are no safety barriers, the ground is soft and it is a long way down. For most of the campaign this post marked the northern point of the Anzac position, although the New Zealanders did establish three outposts north of Walker's Ridge to watch for a Turkish attack from the north.

What happened here? On the morning of 25 April, groups of men who had landed at North Beach (Stand 1) climbed up to Walker's Ridge and moved onto The Nek (Stand 11), Baby 700 (Stand 12b) and beyond. Walker's Ridge formed Anzac's northern perimeter and, for most of the campaign, was developed and held by New Zealanders.

That first night after the landing, the Turkish *2nd Battalion* attacked the ridge constantly from the north. The Turks suffered a distinct disadvantage. A mixed batch of Australians and New Zealanders defended the ridge and were expecting an attack. The Turks were forced to assault up the ridge in the dark. By morning the enemy battalion had been destroyed and Walker's Ridge remained in Allied hands. Some of those at rest in the Walker's Ridge Cemetery were killed in this attack. Another attempt by the Turks to retake the ridge occurred on 30 June and was successfully defeated by the 8th and 9th Light Horse Regiments.

View north from Walker's Ridge looking towards the Commonwealth War Graves workshops and Outpost 1, and showing the Anzacs' clear advantage which allowed them to repel the Turkish attacks against this position on the night of 25 April.

The evacuation. Walk to the viewing area opposite the Sphinx and look down on Stand 1 – North Beach. Directly opposite where the commemorative wall now stands, a long pier (Williams' Pier) once stood. Several smaller piers were located nearby. It was from these piers over the nights of 19 and 20 December 1915 that the majority of Anzacs finally left the Peninsula.

In October, General Sir Ian Hamilton, the Allied commander, was replaced by General Sir Charles Monro. Monro immediately conducted a survey of the situation and reported to London. In his report, Monro summarised the position at Anzac, writing:

The Force, in short, held a line possessing every possible military defect. The position was without depth, the communications were insecure and dependent on the weather. No means existed for the concealment and deployment of fresh troops destined for the offensive— whilst the Turks enjoyed full powers of observation, abundant Artillery positions, and they had been given the time to supplement the natural advantages which the position presented by all the devices at the disposal of the Field Engineer.

He also found the troops inadequately supplied and prepared for a winter offensive, a shortage of artillery ammunition, much sickness and 'a very grave dearth of officers competent to take command of men'. He concluded that a 'complete evacuation was the only wise course to pursue'. Field Marshal Kitchener, Secretary of State for War, was unconvinced and made his own visit to Gallipoli in November. He quickly arrived at the same conclusion. Kitchener's initial reluctance to evacuate was, in part, due to the massive difficulty in evacuating over fourteen divisions, most of which were in close proximity to the enemy. Secrecy would be almost impossible and thousands of casualties were expected.

As winter set in, troop numbers on Anzac dwindled and the forward troops gradually reduced their hostile actions, developing various ruses to trick the Turks into thinking they were simply settling into a winter routine. For example, all troops maintained long periods of complete silence, but would react aggressively when the Turks came to investigate. Others played cricket on Shell Green to convince the Turks that life was proceeding as normal.

The Anzac drip rifle. During the evacuation, hundreds of rifles all along the Anzac front were rigged with two mess tins. A simple but ingenious device, the top mess tin was filled with water with a hole in the bottom to allow water to drip into the other mess tin. This second tin was attached to the trigger and, as it filled with water, its weight would eventually fire the rifle. By adjusting the size of the hole in the first tin, the rifles could be set to discharge at different intervals, anywhere from a few minutes to several hours. *(Artwork by Jeff Isaacs)*

As the evacuation date approached, the Anzacs rigged an ingenious device that enabled rifles to fire along the trench-line without anyone pulling the trigger. This meant that the forward trenches could be gradually emptied; leaving only a few men to rig the devices and trick the Turks into thinking the trenches were still fully manned.

Unlike most of the operations at Gallipoli, the evacuation was extremely well planned and executed. It was a complete success. Much of the credit for this belongs to Anzac's Chief of Staff, Australian Brigadier Brudenell White, whose planning for the withdrawal was 'meticulous'. Over two nights, 41,000 men were evacuated from Anzac. Many tied rags, old clothes or sandbags around their shoes to muffle their steps. On the Turkish side, the surprise was total. While most senior Allied officers agreed with Monro and Kitchener that there was no viable alternative to evacuation, the decision did not rest easy with the men. Most were bitter at having to leave their dead mates behind. One soldier pointed to a cemetery and remarked to General Birdwood as he passed, 'I hope **they** won't hear us marching down the deres [valleys].'

Things to see. The cemetery was fashioned during the occupation and consists of two plots separated by what used to be a wide communications

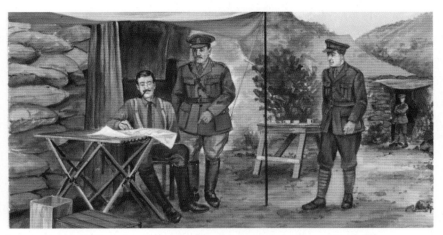

Brigadier Brudenell White plans the evacuation of Anzac from his dugout near Anzac Cove. *(Artwork by Jeff Isaacs)*

trench that ran up to The Nek. Today, 92 men are either buried or commemorated in this cemetery. Wander through the cemetery and note the date on many of the headstones. Remarkably, a number of men came straight up these almost sheer cliff faces from the beach on 25 April, only to be killed in their first engagement with the enemy. Buried here is Trooper Harold Rush, a young West Australian farmhand from the 10th Light Horse Regiment. Knowing he was about to die in the third wave of the assault at The Nek, he turned to his mate beside him and said, 'Goodbye cobber. God bless you.' Later, his mother had these words inscribed on his headstone. (As you walk into the cemetery, look for the small PLOT 2 sign. His grave is directly in front of the sign - II.C.4.) Also buried here are several men

from the 8th and 10th Light Horse Regiments who, seriously wounded in the charge at The Nek on 7 August, died of their wounds on Walker's Ridge. Walk to the northern side of the ridge just opposite the cemetery and take in the views north to Suvla Bay. (The red tiled buildings immediately below you belong to the Commonwealth War Graves Commission workshop.)

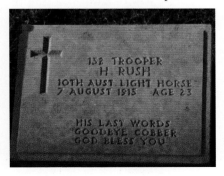

Headstone of Trooper Rush at Walker's Ridge Cemetery.

OPTIONAL WALK 12A - RUSSELL'S TOP

Duration: 40 mins round trip.
Distance: 200-400 m.
Difficulty: Medium to Hard – depending on vegetation.

About 50 metres back along the track to The Nek Cemetery, you will notice two trails leading off to the right (depending on how high the vegetation is). Either of these trails (neither one is marked) will lead you over the crest of Russell's Top. On the day of the landing, small groups of Australians managed to make their way up and over Plugge's Plateau (Stand 5), across the Razor Edge, along Russell's Top (Stand 12a) and onto The Nek (Stand 11). Others climbed up to Russell's Top in an attempt to confront the enemy. Those who first moved over Russell's Top did so in a bayonet charge to clear the withdrawing enemy from this dominating position. They found a flat area about 400 metres long by 50 metres wide amid the sharp peaks and cliffs that typify the area. When the Kiwis arrived in the afternoon they immediately made their way along Monash Valley and Russell's Top to reinforce The Nek. By then, however, the fighting all along the front had become bloody and intense. Baby 700 had been retaken by the Turks and they had good observation over The Nek, Russell's Top and even Plugge's

Plateau. Turkish artillery began to shell Russell's Top just as the Kiwis were attempting to make their way to reinforce the Australian line. Many were killed or wounded. For the rest of the campaign, Russell's Top became an important depth and reserve position from which machine-guns could buttress the forward positions at The Nek, Pope's Hill and Quinn's Post. It also remained a dangerous location as it was always under enemy observation and fire.

OPTIONAL WALK 12B - BABY 700 CEMETERY (22.2KM)

Duration: 15 mins **Distance:** 200 m from the Nek. **Difficulty:** Easy.

Walk or drive back up past The Nek and onto the main road. About 200 metres further along the road (heading north) you will come to the entrance of the Baby 700 Cemetery on the right-hand side of the road. This area was named after the hill just behind the cemetery and was occupied by the Turks for almost the entire campaign. From here you can see the excellent fields of fire the Turks had along almost the entire Anzac front. On the morning of the landing, a few officers and their men from the 11th and 12th Battalions reached this point before being stopped by the Turks coming down from the direction of Chunuk Bair. A few small groups, most notably Captain Eric Tulloch and some men from his 11th Battalion, went further on towards Battleship Hill, but were forced to withdraw to where you are now standing as Turkish resistance increased. Buried here is Captain Joseph Lalor, 12th Battalion, aged 30 (Plot Special Memorial No.4). Lalor was the grandson of Peter Lalor, leader of the Eureka Rebellion at Ballarat in 1854. He was killed in action leading a charge at Baby 700 carrying, so legend decrees, his grandfather's sword. The men buried in this cemetery were killed in that first day's fighting and include troops from the 1st, 2nd, 11th, 12th, 16th, Auckland and Canterbury battalions.

Mustafa Kemal's Monument.

STAND 13 - CHUNUK BAIR (23.7 KM)

Direction to the stand. As you approach Chunuk Bair, you will see a parking area. Park your car here and walk up to the Turkish Monument (see picture).

New Zealand Monument at Chunuk Bair.

The terrain. You are now standing on one of the most dominant hills in the Anzac area, and a key objective of the New Zealanders during the August offensive. Unfortunately for the Anzacs, Chunuk Bair remained in Turkish hands for almost the entire campaign. Wander around the area north of the Turkish Monument (where the reconstructed trenches are). From here you have a clear view as far away as Suvla Bay. Now walk to the western edge of Chunuk Bair—you may need to battle the undergrowth a little but the view is worth the effort. From here you can see back towards North Beach and south-west along the Sari Bair range. Chunuk Bair provides an excellent position from which to observe much of the Anzac front line. Even those without a basic appreciation of the way the military regards terrain cannot but be impressed by the crucial nature of this piece of ground. Indeed, Mustafa Kemal recognised it as his vital ground and moved to occupy it as soon as he learnt of the Anzac landings around Ari Burnu.

What happened here? Around 10.00 a.m. on 25 April, Mustafa Kemal and the advance elements of his division arrived atop this hill, Chunuk Bair (or *Conkbayiri*). Chunuk Bair was a key objective of the Anzacs on the day of the landing and, despite valiant attempts to take and occupy the heights, it remained firmly in Turkish hands.

Because of the strength of the Turkish positions between Chunuk Bair and the Anzac front, the Allies came closest to capturing this position during the August offensive. A large Anzac force was committed to the attack in support of the British landings at Suvla. At dawn on 8 August, the New Zealand Wellington Battalion made it to the summit and was staggered by its panoramic views and clear observation of almost the entire Anzac battlefield.

They had little time to enjoy the view, however, as the Turks were determined to throw the Kiwis off the hill. Throughout that day the Wellingtons, reinforced by parties from the Auckland and Otago Battalions and the Wellington Mounted Rifles, hung on against determined Turkish attacks. 'Of the 760 Wellington Battalion men who had captured the height that morning', wrote Charles Bean, 'there came out only 70 unwounded or slightly wounded men.' They were relieved by a British battalion late on 9 August, but the position was retaken soon after. Other Kiwis hung on through 9 August, but were eventually either killed or forced to retire.

Had the attack on Chunuk Bair succeeded it could have altered the course of the campaign. But, like so many of the grand ideas for Gallipoli, this attack proved overly optimistic and poorly planned. In this instance it was a complicated plan that had three separate forces moving over different routes and across difficult and unfamiliar terrain at night. Notwithstanding the complexity of the plan, the Anzacs still had to deal with the courage and tenacity of the Turkish *57th Regiment* and the outstanding leadership of Mustafa Kemal. The performance of Kemal and his Mehmets on 10 August arguably saved the Ottoman Empire.

Things to see. If you have not done so already, take a look at the New Zealand National Memorial. This is the main New Zealand memorial on Gallipoli and is designed to be seen from all of the key New Zealand battlefields on Anzac. About 50 metres south of this memorial is a reconstructed trench-line. This is part of the line held by the New Zealand Wellington Battalion during the fierce fighting on this summit on 8 August. Now walk through the cemetery. Of the 632 Commonwealth soldiers buried here, only ten have been identified. Most were buried by the Turks after the August offensive. Note the lone gravestone to Private Punahang Limbu of the 10th Gurkha Rifles who was killed here on 10 August. The 10th Gurkhas, part of the 29th Indian Infantry Brigade, was just one of the Allied regiments that participated in the attack on Chunuk Bair. By the end of the campaign, the 10th Gurkhas had lost 75% of its officers and over 40% of its other ranks.

Finally, go to the south-west side of the cemetery. This is the New Zealand Memorial Wall and carries the names of 852 New Zealanders who died assaulting this range and whose graves are unknown. Named here (Panel 17) is Lieutenant Colonel William Malone. Malone was the Commanding Officer of the Wellington Battalion and led his men in numerous charges against the Turks on this hill until he was killed on 8 August.

Lone grave of Gurkha soldier at Chunuk Bair Cemetery.

OPTIONAL WALK 13A – TRACK TO THE FARM CEMETERY

Duration: 20 mins one-way. **Distance:** 550 m. **Difficulty:** Medium -Hard – very steep on return.

Just south of the summit (near the kiosks) is a fire break that runs west along Rhododendron Ridge, with a wooden CWGC sign indicating the direction to the Farm Cemetery. This ridge was used by the New Zealanders as their line of attack for their assaults on Chunuk Bair on 7 and 8 August. Walk down this fire break about 100 metres until you see another sign pointing you to a path off to the right. This is where the path becomes more of a track and there is a steep decline. Do not attempt this walk if you are not at least in reasonable physical shape. After about a fifteen minutes' walk you will emerge onto a small plateau. Continue to follow the path until you arrive at the Farm Cemetery.

Sign to the Farm.

The Farm was named after a stone shepherd's hut that once existed on the plateau. While parties of New Zealanders passed this spot during their assaults on Chunuk Bair, it was not occupied until 10 August when the British 39th Brigade, supported by some Kiwis, arrived here. It was to be a short stay. On the morning of 10 August the Allied front on this plateau was about 400 metres north-east of the cemetery and held by the 9th Worcesters. The Turks, having cleared Chunuk Bair, now poured down the slope and overwhelmed those holding the Farm plateau. The Worcesters' diary recorded that 'For some three hours a desperate struggle raged . . . when nearly all the officers and most of the men were down, the remnant of the 39th Brigade fell back to the more sheltered position in the dead ground at the head of the ravine.' The Turks then occupied this plateau for the remainder of the campaign. The Farm Cemetery was constructed in 1919 and contains 652 burials from this area, of which only seven are identified. The views from the plateau are magnificent and well worth the walk.

STAND 14 – HILL 60 (BOMBA TEPE)

Direction to the stand. Approximately 4.2 kilometres from North Beach Commemorative Site.

The Hill 60 Cemetery is located about 4.2 kilometres from the North Beach Commemorative Site. It is clearly marked by a CWGC brown, wooden sign on the main road to the Suvla area. The route to the cemetery is via a rough track on your right, which is about 700 metres long. Note that this track can be difficult to negotiate in the wet and your car can become quickly bogged.

The terrain. The cemetery is located on the southern slope of the hill which a combined British, Australian, New Zealand and Gurkha force attacked between 21 and 29 August in what Bean described 'as one of the most difficult in which Australian troops were ever engaged.' The hill itself

View from Hill 60 towards Chunuk Bair. The Chunuk Bair monument and Turkish flag is just visible on the skyline

is surprisingly small. However, its possession by the Turks was preventing the Anzac and Suvla positions from linking up. Hill 60 is part of a low range that links to the heights to your south-west. From the cemetery you can clearly see Chunuk Bair (see picture), Hill Q and Hill 971.

A Turkish trench line ran through this location and extended north-west and north-east, with both ends curving up to the heights above. The attack on 21 August saw the main thrust coming from the south by Monash's 4th Australian Brigade and the New Zealand Mounted Rifles, while the Connaught Rangers and Indian Brigade assaulted from the south-west. The 18th Australian Battalion attacked

from the west on the following day.

What happened here? After the failure of the August offensive to take the heights of Hill 971 and Chunuk Bair, it was necessary to take two lower hills, the possession of which by the Turks was preventing the Anzac and Suvla beachheads from linking up. These positions were Scimitar Hill and Hill 60. The battle for Hill 60, the last major assault at Gallipoli, was planned to coincide with an assault by General Stopford's British IX Corps on Scimitar Hill.

The main attack force for Hill 60 was based on Brigadier John Monash's 4th Brigade, supported by elements of the 29th Indian Brigade, the New Zealand Mounted Rifle Brigade and three

British battalions. However, many of these units had been involved in the battles of early August and were understrength and weakened by disease. Monash's infantry opened the attack on 21 August but were given no artillery support, and met stiff resistance from the entrenched enemy. Supported by the Indian Brigade, some troops eventually managed to gain a foothold at the base of the hill, but they had suffered many casualties soon became pinned down. To make matters even worse the undergrowth had caught fire in the afternoon, burning to death a number of the wounded.

Private Joseph Walden, 18th Battalion, was killed on 22 August while attacking Hill 60. Like many members of the battalion who were killed that day, Walden had been in Gallipoli for just three days. He is commemorated on the Lone Pine Memorial to the missing. (AWM H05799)

The battle continued the following day with the arrival fresh reinforcements in the form of the Australian 18th Battalion. This battalion was part of the newly arrived 2nd Australian Division which, while fresh, healthy and keen, was inexperienced and poorly equipped. This showed in the conduct and results of this, their first attack, when they were ordered to assault with bayonet only and lost nearly 400 men with little to show for it. Over one thousand allied troops were either killed or wounded in the first forty-eight hours of the battle.

Late on the afternoon of 27 August the attack resumed with all the allied troops available, including the British battalions, New Zealand mounted rifles, 18th Australian Battalion and the 4th Brigade. Most of these units and formations had been involved in the earlier fighting and were understrength with many of their men nursing wounds. While this force made some headway, they were facing stiff resistance, suffering high casualty rates and, consequently, the attack was at risk of bogging down. In an attempt to regain the momentum, elements of the 3rd Light Horse Brigade were committed later that night. It ended in near disaster when two groups of the 9th Light Horse Regiment were decimated by enemy fire and counter attacks, and the death of their Commanding Officer, Lieutenant-Colonel Reynell.

Further bloody attempts to capture the hill occurred until 29 August when the offensive ceased. While some enemy trenches were captured, enabling the Suvla and Anzac positions to link up, they failed to take the summit. The battle for Hill 60 showed that the Allies had failed to learn the lessons of their earlier battles. The assault was poorly planned and coordinated, with inadequate artillery support, bad maps and intelligence, and no reconnaissance. The casualty rates also resembled earlier battles with the 4th Brigade's combat strength being reduced from over four thousand to fewer than one thousand.

Things to see. The Hill 60 cemetery contains 788 graves, of which only 76 are identified. Thirty Australians are buried or commemorated here, twenty of them from either the 18th Battalion or the 9th Light Horse Regiment. Almost immediately after the battle some trenches cutting through the existing cemetery were used to bury those killed. In 1919 the War Graves Commission added others to this cemetery from smaller actions in these foothills. This cemetery also contains one of only four New Zealand memorials on the Gallipoli peninsula commemorating New Zealanders who have no known grave.

This memorial bears the names of 183 New Zealanders missing from the attacks on Hill 60.

Look for Special Memorial 4 - Lieutenant-Colonel Reynell, Commanding Officer of the 9th Light Horse Regiment, who was killed 28 August leading a charge against the Turkish trench line on Hill 60.

OPTIONAL DRIVE 14A - SECOND BATTLE OF KRITHIA.

Duration: 20 mins drive one-way.
Distance: 15.4 km.

Battlefield Museum at Alçitepe.

Direction to the area. To locate the Krithia battlefields, start at the Kabatepe Museum intersection, just south of Brighton Beach. Follow the signs to the Kum Hotel (six kilometres) and then to Alçitepe (the current name for Krithia). After about 14 kilometres you will reach a T intersection in Alçitepe. You will know you are at the right place because there is an interesting military museum on your left at the intersection. The museum is worth a quick visit.

As you leave the museum, reset your car's odometer as your destination, the Redoubt Cemetery, is about 2 kilometres from the museum. Turn left at the intersection, drive through the main street of town and turn right at the end of the road. Follow this road while keeping right at road junctions. As you approach 2 kilometres from the town, keep an eye out for a sign to the Redoubt Cemetery and a tree-lines track on your right. Walk down this track about 300 metres to the cemetery. You are now in the vicinity of the front line for the 2nd Battle of Krithia.

What happened here? As the Australian and New Zealanders were landing around Anzac Cove on 25 April, other British formations were landing at Cape Helles on the southern point of the Gallipoli Peninsula. Their objective was the Kilitbahir plateau, but determined Turkish opposition had restricted their beachhead as it had for the Anzacs. The first battle of Krithia, on 28 April was an attempt to break out of this confined beachhead. While they gained some ground, it proved a disaster for the British 29th Division. Its commander, Major General Hunter-Weston, appeared indifferent to casualties and convinced Hamilton that 'one more attack should do it'. Consequently, Hamilton asked Birdwood for troops to support the decimated 29th Division.

In response to Hamilton's request for troops, Birdwood sent a composite Anzac division comprising the 2nd Australian Infantry Brigade and

Charge of the 2nd Infantry Brigade at Krithia. *(AWM ART09558)*

160

the New Zealand Infantry Brigade. Arriving on 6 May, the Anzacs were initially held in reserve and given little information about the planned attack. They were committed on 8 May, almost at the last minute, without either detailed orders or a proper briefing. There was neither time to conduct any reconnaissance nor to familiarise the troops with the ground over which they would attack. In true Hunter-Weston style the plan was simple: a daylight frontal assault across open ground against a well-prepared and fortified enemy. The Australians, while gaining the most ground that day, lost over 1,000 men in about thirty minutes. The New Zealanders suffered 835 killed or wounded that afternoon. All up, about a third of the attacking force, or

6,000 men, were lost. Poor operational planning by Hunter-Weston's staff also increased the death toll among his own men. Many of the wounded could not be treated in time to save their lives as no casualty collection stations had been organised; there were too few stretcher-bearers, ambulances or wagons to carry the wounded to the beach; and, once at the beach, little had been done to arrange for the wounded to be ferried to the hospital ships, or even for the hospital ships to be prepared for battle casualties. Notwithstanding the disaster of the two battles for Krithia, Hunter-Weston was promoted to lieutenant general on 24 May, given command of the British VIII Corps and launched yet another disastrous attack on 4 June in the Third Battle of Krithia. This

THE HELLES WAR ZONE

The Helles war zone, 1915, showing the location of the Helles Memorial, and the Redoubt, Twelve Tree Copse and Lancashire Landing Cemeteries (*http://en.wikipedia.org/wiki/Second_Battle_of_Krithia*)

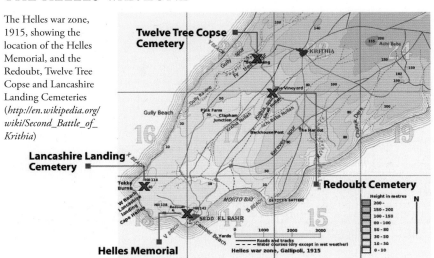

third attack was no more successful than the previous two but it still cost the British and French battalions involved a further 6,500 casualties. Hunter-Weston was invalided from Gallipoli in July suffering from nervous exhaustion.

Things to see. The Redoubt Cemetery takes its name from the chain of forts made by the Turks across the southern end of the peninsula in the fighting for Krithia and the Redoubt Line on which the advance halted in May. Buried just to the right inside the gate is Lieutenant-Colonel Robert Gartside who, on 8 May 1915, was the Commanding Officer of the 7th Australian Battalion. Gartside was killed by machine-gun fire during the Australian advance as he rose to lead a charge, shouting 'Come on, boys, I know it's deadly but we must go on'. He is allegedly the first man buried in the Redoubt Cemetery when it was first build by members of the 2nd Australian Brigade after the attack.

The cemetery itself is a relatively large one. Located here are 2,027 graves, less than 20 per cent of which are identified. It was used throughout the remainder of the campaign, with additional bodies added after the war when the battlefields were cleared.

OPTIONAL DRIVE 14B – OTHER BRITISH, NEW ZEALAND AND TURKISH CEMETERIES AND MEMORIALS

Çanakkale Martyrs' Memorial (*Çanakkale Sehitleri Aniti*). From the Redoubt Cemetery continue to follow the road south-west towards Helles. After about 1.5 kilometres look for a sharp turn-off to the left to the Skew bridge. Soon after, the road forks. Take the right-hand fork while watching for the signs to *Çanakkale Sehitleri Aniti*. By this time you should be able to see the massive, towering memorial high on a hill near the coast. Built in the 1950s at the head of Morto Bay and overlooking the Dardanelles, the Çanakkale Martyrs' Memorial is the largest memorial on the Peninsula. It is Turkey's tribute to the bravery and sacrifice of over 86,000 Turkish soldiers. The location of the memorial is a reminder to visiting Australians and New Zealanders that, for Turkey, the Gallipoli campaign was about more than just the Anzac front, or even the British and French landings. To the Turks, it was primarily about control of the Dardanelles. Indeed, the key date for celebrating their victory in the Çanakkale War is 18 March, not 25 April, as it was in March 1915 that Turkey defeated the combined French and Royal Navies. There is also an interesting museum located near the memorial.

Çanakkale Martyrs' Memorial.

Helles Memorial. From the Çanakkale Martyrs' Memorial go back the way you came. After crossing the Skew Bridge again, turn left at the main road. The Helles Memorial is about 3.6 kilometres from the Skew Bridge and 5.5 kilometres from the Çanakkale Martyrs' Memorial. The area is well signed and, as you approach Cape Helles, you cannot miss the thirty-metre-high obelisk towering over you as you approach. The main inscription on the memorial reads:

The Helles Memorial is both a memorial to the Gallipoli campaign and to the 20,763 men who fell in that campaign and whose graves are unknown or who were lost or buried

at sea in Gallipoli waters. Inscribed on it are the names of all the ships that took part in the campaign and the titles of the army formations and units which served on the Peninsula together with the names of 18,985 sailors, soldiers and marines from the United Kingdom, 248 soldiers from Australia, and 1,530 soldiers of the Indian Army.

The 248 Australian names recorded here are men from the 2nd Infantry Brigade who fought and died at the 2nd Battle of Krithia in early May 1915 and have no known grave. Also listed at Helles are the main military units of the Australian Imperial Force (AIF) and the NZ Expeditionary Force (NZEF) which fought at Gallipoli.

Helles Memorial

'V' Beach. Once you have finished at the Helles Memorial, walk down the path, through the vendor stalls, to the Ertuğrul Fort and the views over 'V' Beach, *SS River Clyde*'s beaching area, and Seddülbahir Fort. During the Allied naval attack on the straits in November 1914, the Seddülbahir Fort was badly damaged and 86 Turkish soldiers killed. For the landings on 25 April 1915, Ertuğrul Cove below was designated by Hamilton's headquarters 'V' Beach and an old steamship *SS River Clyde* was run aground packed with British soldiers. Holes had been cut in the steel hull to provide sally ports from which the troops would emerge onto gangways and then to a bridge of smaller boats linking the ship to the beach. The ship, intended as a floating version of the Trojan horse, was designed to offer the soldiers some protection for their landing. However, everything that could go wrong did go wrong and, as observed by a passing Allied airman, 'the water of the bay ran red with blood'. Having taken severe casualties, the remaining men on board waited until nightfall to storm the beach and, eventually, capture the forts.

Six Victoria Crosses were awarded in the first few hours of the landing.

Lancashire Landing Cemetery. This cemetery is approximately 2 kilometres from the Helles Memorial and is on your left on a cliff just above 'W' Beach where the 1st Lancashire Fusiliers landed under very severe fire on 25 April and won '6 VCs before breakfast'. 'W' Beach was a particularly dangerous spot for a landing as it was well defended by the Turks with interlocking arcs of machine-guns, mines and wire entanglements. The German advisers to the Turks thought this beach impregnable. Buried or commemorated here are 1,237 men, 135 of whom are unknown. Included in these figures are 27 Australians and 15 New Zealanders who were wounded during the 2nd Battle of Krithia and died at the Advanced Dressing Station that was established near here.

Should you wish to visit the beach, you

Seddülbahir Fort from the Ertuğrul Fort, showing the area where the *SS River Clyde* was beached (near the line of exposed rocks) and the 'V' Beach Cemetery in the foreground.

will need to head back the way you have just come about 700 metres until you come to a track off to the right (west). Follow this downhill but note that, while the road is passable most of the year, it can become boggy and the sharp thorn bushes on the road's edge can scratch your car. Walk to the beach and you can easily see the clear advantage enjoyed by the defenders of the cove, and the massive task of the 'Lancs' in overcoming them.

Just one of the 27 Australian soldiers buried at the Lancashire Landing Cemetery.

Pink Farm Cemetery. About 3.5 kilometres from the Lancashire Landing Cemetery is the Pink Farm Cemetery. Follow the sign down a short track on your right. Pink Farm (or more properly *Sotiri Farm*) was a building close to the site of the attacks on Krithia. Buried or commemorated in this cemetery are 602 servicemen, of whom 438 have been identified, including three Australians and five New Zealanders. A special memorial commemorates a further 219 casualties known or believed to be buried here.

Twelve Tree Copse Cemetery. From Pink Farm continue along the road towards Alçitepe about 3 kilometres. The Twelve Tree Copse Cemetery, on your left and well signposted, is named after a nearby topographical feature and was established following the Armistice with the incorporation of the numerous isolated gravesites and small burial grounds from the Krithia battles. The cemetery contains, or commemorates the names of, 3,360 servicemen, including twelve Australians and eighty New Zealanders. Of these, 2,226 are unidentified. The cemetery also contains the Twelve Tree Copse (New Zealand) Memorial, one of four memorials erected to commemorate New Zealand soldiers who fell on the Gallipoli Peninsula and whose graves are not known. The memorial relates to engagements outside the limits of Anzac in which New Zealand soldiers took part. It bears almost 180 names.

Returning. When you leave the Twelve Tree Copse Cemetery, you have the option of returning to Anzac or driving back towards Çanakkale. Firstly, continue on to Alçitepe, heading north. As you enter the town you will come to that T intersection with the small battlefield museum. Pass the museum and about two kilometres from the town you will come to another intersection. Take the left fork to return to Kabatepe and the Anzac battlefields, or the right fork if you are heading to Kilitbahir, Eceabat or Çanakkale (signed to Behramli).

OPTIONAL DRIVE 14C – ATATURK'S COMMAND HEADQUARTERS, BIGALI

Duration: 15 mins drive one-way.
Distance: 10.5 km.

From the Kabatepe Museum, drive back towards Eceabat. As you pass the Gelibolu Information Centre, and just before the main coast road to Eceabat, look for a turn to your left (about 6.5 kilometres from the Kabatepe Museum intersection or 4 kilometres from Eceabat). It is signposted to *Bigali* & *Atatürk Evi*. About 2 kilometres along this road, turn left for Bigali. After another 2.5 kilometres you will arrive in Bigali's town square. There is a small museum off this square. While the museum is small, the village was recently renovated and the townsfolk take great delight in showing off their village to foreign visitors. After a visit

to the museum, take in a coffee at the café in the square and meet some of the locals. They are very friendly and the coffee is good.

After coffee, ask directions to *Atatürk Evi* (Ataturk's house). Everyone will be more than willing to point you in the right direction as it was here on 25 April 1915 that Colonel Mustafa Kemal, Commander of the *19th Division*, was living when news arrived of the 'English' landings at Ari Burnu.

Opposite page, left: An Australian senior officer at Gallipoli. Australian officers generally wore tailor-made uniforms and carried a pistol and field glasses (binoculars). The classic British Sam Brown belt was standard 'rig', as were leather gaiters or riding boots. (*Artwork by Jeff Isaacs*)

Opposite page, right: An Australian private soldier at Gallipoli. Prior to the landing at Gallipoli, every Australian soldier was inspected to ensure that he had all his equipment, which included a rifle, bayonet, backpack, two empty sandbags, a full water bottle, 200 rounds of ammunition and two days' rations. (*Artwork by Jeff Isaacs*)

The Ataturk Museum in Bigali.

BIBLIOGRAPHY

Ashmead-Bartlett, E., *The Uncensored Dardanelles*, Hutchinson & Co., London, 1928

Bean, C.E.W., *Official History of Australia in the War of 1914–18. Vols I & II: The Story of Anzac*, 7th edn., Angus & Robertson, Sydney, 1937

Burness, P., *The Nek: The Tragic Charge of the Light Horse at Gallipoli*, Kangaroo Press, Sydney, 1996

Cameron, D.W., *25 April 1915: The Day the Anzac Legend was Born*, Allan & Unwin, Sydney, 2007

Carlyon, L., *Gallipoli*, Pan Macmillan, Sydney, 2001

Evans, M., *From Legend to Learning: Gallipoli and the Military Revolution of World War I*, Land Warfare Studies Centre, Working Paper No.110, Canberra, April 2000

Fewster, K., Basarin, H. & Basarin, V., *A Turkish View of Gallipoli / Çanakkale*, Hodja Educational Resources Cooperative Ltd., Melbourne, 1985

——, *Gallipoli: The Turkish Story*, Allen & Unwin, Sydney, 2003

Gilbert, M., *The Straits of War: Gallipoli Remembered*, Sutton Publications, Cornwall, 2000

Haythornthwaite, P.J., *Gallipoli 1915: Frontal Assault on Turkey*, Osprey Publications, UK, 1991

King, J., *Gallipoli Diaries*, Kangaroo Press, Sydney, 2003

Macklin, R., *Jacka VC*, Allen & Unwin, Sydney, 2006

Moorehead, A., *Gallipoli*, Arrow Books, London, 1959

Pedersen, P., *The Anzacs: Gallipoli to the Western Front*, Penguin Group, Melbourne, 2007

Levine, L.A., *Frommer's Turkey*, 4th edn., Wiley Publications, New Jersey, 2006

Stanley, P., *Quinn's Post, Anzac, Gallipoli*, Allen & Unwin, Sydney, 2005

Travers, T., *Gallipoli 1915*, Tempus Publications, London, 2004

Williams, P., *The Battle for Anzac Ridge 25 April 1915*, Australian Military History Publications, 2007

Wright, T., *Turn Right at Istanbul: A Walk on the Gallipoli Peninsula*, Allen & Unwin, Sydney, 2003

Yale, P., Carillet, J., Maxwell, V., & Raphael, M., *Turkey*, 7th edn., Lonely Planet Publications, UK.

Good Tour Books

Holt, Major and Mrs, *Battlefield Guide to Gallipoli*, Pen & Sword, London, 2000

Taylor, P., & Cupper, P., *Gallipoli: A Battlefield Guide*, 2nd edn., Kangaroo Press, Sydney, 1989

Internet Sites of Note

History

http://www.anzacsite.gov.au Department of Veterans' Affairs-sponsored website giving a good overview of the Gallipoli campaign, offers some good advice about attending Anzac Day at Gallipoli and provides links to sound files, etc.

http://www.anzac.govt.nz Good for a New Zealand perspective on the campaign.

Tracing relatives who served

http://www.cwgc.org Contains details on 1.7 million men and women of the Commonwealth forces who died during the two world wars and the 23,000 cemeteries, memorials and other locations worldwide where they are commemorated.

http://www.dva.gov.au Department of Veterans' Affairs website. From here you can research an Australian relative who served in the war, or find current information on Anzac Day commemorations (including those at Gallipoli).

http://www.naa.gov.au National Archives of Australia website. Another good website for researching relatives who served in the Australian forces.

Visiting Gallipoli

http://www.turkeytravelplanner.com An excellent site with lots of information for travellers to Turkey.

http://www.anzacsite.gov.au

http://user.glo.be/~snelders/contents.html

http://www.anzac.govt.nz/gallipoliguide/index.html

http://www.travelturkey.com

http://www.lonelyplanet.com For some common sense tips.

http://www.frommers.com/destinations/turkey

Where to stay

http://www.anzacgallipolitours.com Part of TJ's Hotel in Eceabat, a good site to book tours and accommodation

http://www.anzachouse.com Website of *Hassle Free Tours,* allows you to book tours, arrange accommodation in the Gallipoli region (mainly Çanakkale) and obtain information on buses to/from Çanakkale and ferry services.

http://www.maydos.com.tr Mid-range hotel in great location at Çanakkale.

http://www.anzachotel.com Two star hotel in good, central location at Çanakkale.

http://www.hotelakol.com.tr Four star Hotel in Çanakkale. Good location. Great views. Good hotel if you can negotiate a room rate to suit your budget.

http://www.gallipoli.com.tr Gallipoli Houses, one of the newest hotels in the area and located very close to the Anzac battlefields

Istanbul

http://www.istanbulcityguide.com What's on in Istanbul, search for a hotel, maps, etc.

Maps

http://www.mapquest.com/maps/map.adp?form type=address&country=TR&addtohistory=&city=Istanbul

Government (Turkish & Australian) travel sites

http://www.turkishembassy.org.au Turkish Embassy, Canberra, website

http://www.smartraveller.gov.au For registering your travel with, and receiving travel advisories from DFAT.

http://www.turizm.gov.tr Turkish Ministry of Tourism website.

http://www.mymerhaba.com Current information on 'what's on in Turkey'

http://www.turkishembassy.org Turkish Embassy, Washington

http://www.tntmagazine.com/gettingstarted for advice on what to take on your trip

INDEX